SPIRITUAL JETSTREAMS

by

Dr. David Huddleston

Table of Contents

Ch. 1. Holy Spirit, My Co-Pilot
Ch. 2. Women And The Holy Spirit
Ch. 3. How To Be Filled With The Holy Spirit
Ch. 4. Slipping Through The Spiritual Jetstream
Ch. 5. Trusting The Spirit Of Jesus
Ch. 6. Total Reliance Upon The Spirit
Ch. 7. Achieving Spiritual Maturity
Ch. 8. Discovering Your Spiritual Gifts
Ch. 9. Marriage And The Spirit

All scripture references are from the
NEW INTERNATIONAL VERSION of the Bible,
copyright 1973, 1978, 1984 by the International Bible
Society unless otherwise noted. All rights reserved.

Copyright © 2003
by Maranatha Ministries International, Inc.
All rights reserved.

Printed in the United States of America.
First printing July 2003.

Biography

Dr. David Huddleston is a former intercontinental airline pilot and has an undergraduate degree from the University of Kentucky along with Master of Divinity and Doctor of Theology degrees from Trinity Seminary. He is the author of *LIFE'S SPIRITUAL INSTRUCTION BOOK* now in its third printing. Dr. Huddleston has preached in over fifty churches in the U.S., Switzerland, Italy, and Jamaica. He lives in Kentucky with his wife of thirty years, Edie, who is an artist. Their grown children, Sean and Heather, live nearby.

Prologue

The following poem, *High Flight*, by John Gillespie Magee, Jr. has had a special meaning for me since I was a child. I would like to begin my book by sharing it with you.

May the Spirit of Jesus Be With You,

David Huddleston,
email: drdavidhuddleston@yahoo.com

High Flight

Oh, I have slipped the surly bonds of earth,
And danced the skies on laughter-silvered wings;
Sunward I've climbed and joined the tumbling mirth
Of sun-split clouds-and done a hundred things
You have not dreamed of-wheeled and soared and swung
High in the sunlit silence. Hov'ring there
I've chased the shouting wind along and flung
My eager craft through footless halls of air,
Up, up the long, delerious burning blue
I've topped the wind-swept heights with easy grace,
Where never lark, or even eagle flew;
And while with silent, lifting mind I've trod
The high untrespassed sanctity of space,
Put out my hand, and touched the face of God.

Pilot Officer John Gillespie Magee, Jr.
No. 412 Squadron, RCAF
Killed in England on 11 December, 1941

Acknowledgements

I would like to thank my wife, Edie,
for the book cover design
and my daughter, Heather,
for countless hours of editing.

This book is dedicated with love to my wife, Edie.

Introduction

Each of us lives our lives in the midst of an invisible spiritual war. We place ourselves in jeopardy when we do not take it seriously (or we simply ignore it). The evangelist Billy Graham has said on many occasions, "Our hearts are never satisfied by materialism." Nevertheless, this generation has embraced materialism to a far greater extent than at any other time in history. Only through our total reliance upon the Holy Spirit as we are lead into a deep and personal relationship with Christ can our hearts ever be truly satisfied. Nothing else will ever suffice. Financial success, a dream home, an expensive SUV, fine clothes or jewelry will not suffice. A fat-free muscular body, sex, power, influence, food, alcohol or drugs will never be sufficient.

According to a recent survey conducted by the Barna Research Group, most Americans who consider themselves to be Christians do not believe in the Holy Spirit or Satan. Sixty-one percent of Americans, including fifty-five percent of those who describe themselves as "born-again" (who have made a "personal commitment to Jesus Christ"), say that "the Holy Spirit is a symbol of God's presence or power, but not a living entity." Barna commented, "We are living amidst the dilution of traditional, Bible-based Christian faith. Millions of Americans are comfortable calling themselves Christian even though their beliefs suggest otherwise. When people who claim to be Christian deny the existence of the Holy Spirit, then we have a people whose Christianity is superficial, compromised, and inconsistent. Perhaps you can say that Americans are religious, but the profile painted by these statistics (thirty-nine percent say Jesus was crucified but never had a physical resurrection, thirty-two percent believe lying is sometimes necessary, and thirty-three percent say looking at pornography is a matter of taste, not morality) suggests that most adults cannot be described as informed about the Christian faith they claim."

      The purpose of my book is to help people to become more aware of the power and presence of the Holy Spirit in their lives and to encourage them to grow toward spiritual maturity through learning to totally rely on the Spirit of God to work out all things for their own good. It is only through this process of spiritual growth and transformation that each of us can become all that God intends for us to be so that we can receive the full blessings from the Lord which are our rightful inheritance.

Spiritual Jetstreams

Chapter 1

Holy Spirit, My Co-Pilot

I must go on boasting. Although there is nothing to be gained, I will go on to visions and revelations from the Lord. I know a man in Christ who fourteen years ago was caught up to the third heaven. Whether it was in the body or out of the body I do not know—God knows. And I know that this man—whether in the body or apart from the body I do not know, but God knows—was caught up to paradise. He heard inexpressible things, things that man is not permitted to tell.

I will boast about a man like that, but I will not boast about myself, except about my weaknesses. Even if I should choose to boast, I would not be a fool, because I would be speaking the truth. But I refrain so no one will think more of me than is warranted by what I do or say. To keep me from becoming conceited because of these surpassingly great revelations, there was given me a thorn in my flesh, a messenger of Satan, to torment me. Three times I pleaded with the Lord to take it away from me. But he said to me, "My grace is sufficient for you, for my power is made perfect in weakness."

Therefore I will boast all the more gladly about my weaknesses, so that Christ's power may rest on me. That is why, for Christ's sake, I delight in weaknesses, in insults, in hardships, in persecutions, in difficulties. For when I am weak, then I am strong.
(2 Cor 12:1-10 NIV)

The Lord said (to Paul), *"My grace is sufficient for you, for my power is made perfect in weakness."*
(2 Cor 12:9a NIV)

David Huddleston

"What's that little red one doing, David?" my mother asked in her typical calm tone as we were on final approach to the small grass runway at my hometown airport of Harrodsburg, Kentucky. She said it so casually that I nearly jerked the yoke out of the airplane when I looked up and saw that we were on a collision course with a Cessna 150. I made a sharp climbing turn to the right to avoid a mid-air collision. Thirty years later, I can still see the pilot's face turned toward the runway in the other plane as he passed in front of us. (He never saw our plane!)

I had just received my private pilot's license at Blue Grass Field in Lexington and thought I was now ready to conquer all the world records in aviation. The skies were mine! I had 35 hours of flight time and I just knew that I was destined to go down in the annals of aviation history as the greatest pilot of all time. I would be the standard against which all future pilots would be measured! NASA would be calling me any day now to replace one of their retiring Mercury astronauts. Chuck Yeager would no doubt ask me for a private lesson.

Since I could now legally carry passengers, I thought it would be a great idea to make my mother my first victim (passenger). I had successfully found the small grass strip in Harrodsburg after an uneventful twenty mile flight from Lexington in my small Cessna trainer and had only bounced the airplane three times on landing. My mother was sitting in her car near the end of the cow pasture (runway) and I thought how impressed she would be with me as I taxied over to pick her up for a sight-seeing trip above our hometown. She looked so proud of my landing and this would be her first flight in a small aircraft.

It was a beautiful spring day with only a few high thin cirrus clouds above 30,000' and visibility was 10 miles. The wind was light and variable out of the northwest as I began a straight-in final approach to runway 31. I had disregarded the standard approach procedure which called for a left downwind leg parallel to the runway and 800' AGL (above ground level) with a 90 degree left turn onto a left base leg while descending. A final 90 degree left turn would have put us on a short final approach for landing to the northwest. This procedure would insure a safe approach and landing for all traffic which might be landing. Since I had never seen anyone use this small airport before, I assumed that I could just approach straight-in for landing. (Anyway, I was in a hurry and had lots of experience!) Also, I had forgotten to monitor the unicom frequency of 122.9 mHz which is to be used for airports without a control tower. The hangar at the Harrodsburg airport had long since ceased to house any aircraft and was now home to the local John Deere dealership. Needless to say, there was no control tower.

It was while we were on short final about 200' AGL that my mother asked about the "little red one" which was turning from a left base onto final approach. I'm not sure she ever realized how close we came to colliding or how STUPID her youngest son was that day. If she did, she never said so and the incident was never mentioned again. I know one of the reasons that God made mothers was surely so they could instill confidence in their nitwit children as they rise to new heights of stupidity on their journey toward maturity.

Praise the Lord for mothers (and for my mother)!

Perhaps you have heard the old saying, "Mid-air collisions may be hazardous to your health." Perhaps you've had a mid-air collision with life. If so, you know that this, too, may be hazardous to your health. Serious physical, emotional, and spiritual problems can result from the stresses placed on the body, mind, and spirit by life's adverse events which we all must go through. You will be tested many times in the days and years ahead and your response each time will either help you to grow stronger or cause you to become weaker depending on how you react.

Robert Urich, the actor who had starred in many popular television series and movies ("Vega$", "Spenser: For Hire"), was speaking on television shortly after learning he had a serious illness. He had been diagnosed with a rare form of cancer which affects the linings of the joints in the body. On the day his physician received the laboratory test results confirming synovial sarcoma, he called Robert to his office and broke the news to him. His doctor told him that radiation and chemotherapy should be initiated immediately and that treatments should begin that afternoon. After much pleading by Robert, the doctor agreed to give him a four-day respite prior to beginning the cancer treatments.

Urich was an avid motorcycle enthusiast and owned a big Harley-Davidson which he enjoyed riding with his wife out in the wide open spaces where they lived. They had decided to go on a trip before beginning his therapy and took off together on the Harley, his wife on the back while he drove. Robert recounted how he had the overwhelming urge as they were riding along to thank God for testing him by allowing this cancer to afflict him. He told how he kept saying over and over, "Thank you, God, for this testing." That's right, he was actually THANKING God for his cancer. He was thanking God for testing him by giving him cancer. Here was this highly successful Hollywood star telling a nationwide TV audience that he was actually thankful for this opportunity that God had given him because he saw it as an opportunity for spiritual growth. He said that he had determined not to feel sorry for himself or to be mad at God but, that he was going to take the "spiritual high road" as he called it and make the best of the situation in which he now found himself. He later told <u>TV Guide</u> that his illness had forced him to rethink what he wanted to do with his "second adulthood" as he called it. He said:

The biggest thing I need to do now is be quiet enough to listen to that inner voice, and that **Spirit of God**. I don't know what's next. I don't want to do the same old stuff, you know? Acting is a melding of intellect and spirit, but basically, it ain't that tough. (Urich eventually succumbed to his illness).

In II Corinthians, Chapter 12, the apostle Paul speaks about the "thorn in my flesh" which was tormenting him. We do not know exactly what this physical problem was but, it was undoubtedly a very painful condition which was bothering Paul a great deal. It has been suggested that perhaps it was an arthritic condition in his joints or maybe an eye problem. Nevertheless, Paul's reaction to his affliction was to take the "spiritual high road" much the same as Robert Urich did. Paul went on to say that he could boast about his weakness because it reminded him of

Christ's power over him. Therefore, he was able to take pleasure in it. Imagine, even though Paul had asked the Lord three times to take this illness away from him and it remained, he was still able to be thankful for his "thorn." God had told Paul, *"My grace is sufficient for you..."* Paul's response was, "OK, if that's the case then I might as well be proud of my disease because when I am weak (physically) then I am really strong (spiritually)." He believed this was because of the power of the Holy Spirit working in his life. And I really believe this is literally true because when we have that inevitable mid-air collision or "near-miss" with life, one of two things will occur: we will either get mad at God for causing this to happen to us and we will become cynical and bitter as we grow apart from his presence, or we will choose to react in a positive way by responding with an attitude of thanksgiving for the Lord to once again demonstrate his love for us and his immense power in our lives. When we react this way, it draws us closer and closer to Jesus as we acknowledge his power over us and our utter helplessness to be in control. Paul wrote, *"Therefore, I will boast all the more gladly about my weaknesses, so that Christ's power may rest on me."*

Following the tragic 1996 crash of TWA Flight 800 in the Atlantic Ocean off Long Island, New York, in which 230 people died, a memorial was dedicated at New York's Kennedy Airport. It was designed by Janet Collett, a TWA flight attendant, in memory of the 54 TWA employees who perished on board the huge Boeing 747 bound from New York to Paris. The sculpture stands six feet tall and consists of a marble base supporting a three-panelled pedestal made of etched green glass. The first panel shows the take-off of a 747 as viewed from behind. The next panel depicts the 747 being cradled in God's hands in mid-air. The last panel shows the metamorphosis of the 747 into a dove being released above the clouds and sun. What a poignant acknowledgment of God's power and grace in our lives!

Watch out for those "little red ones" out there (life's experiences). The next one might be headed straight for you! Your reaction will determine if it's a mid-air collision or a "near-miss." **If you will let the Holy Spirit be your co-pilot** then you'll never have to worry about a safe trip!

David Huddleston

Spiritual Jetstreams

Chapter 2

Women and The Holy Spirit

Then God commanded, "Let the earth produce all kinds of animal life: domestic and wild, large and small." And it was done. So God made them all and he was pleased with what he saw. Then God said, "And now we will make human beings. They will be like us and resemble us. They will have power over the fish, the birds, and all animals, domestic and wild, large and small."

So God created human beings, making them to be like himself. He created them male and female, blessed them and said, "Have many children so that your descendants will live all over the earth and bring it under their control. I am putting you in charge of the fish, the birds, and all the wild animals. I have provided all kinds of grain and all kinds of fruit for you to eat. But for all the wild animals and for all the birds I have provided grass and leafy plants for food." And it was done. God looked at everything he had made and he was very pleased. Evening passed and morning came. That was the sixth day.
(Genesis 1:24-31 TEV)

So there is no difference between Jews and Gentiles, between slaves and free men, between men and women; you are all one in union with Christ Jesus. If you belong to Christ, then you are the descendants of Abraham and will receive what God has promised.
(Galatians 3:28-29 TEV)

"The ceiling is 500 feet, overcast, visibility one mile in heavy rain, temperature 87 degrees. Winds are 070 degrees at 18 knots with gusts to 25 knots," the second officer advised as we began our descent into the "ring of fire" surrounding La Aurora International Airport at Guatemala City, Guatemala. It was nearly midnight and we were all anxious to get to our hotel for a few hours of rest before returning to Miami at 0800 the next day. Our flight had brought us from Miami down over Key West, then Cozumel on the Yucatan Peninsula before heading down over Belize and beginning our descent into Guatemala City. It was a spectacular sight at night due to the ring of active volcanoes encircling La Aurora International. The fact that these volcanic peaks were all above the runway elevation gave the sensation of descending into a black hole surrounded by a ring of fire in order to make the approach for landing at La Aurora, which has an elevation of 4952 feet above sea level. Since the airport was constructed with the approach end much higher than the rest of the runway, the landing there required a quick and somewhat firm touchdown prior to going down a long, sloping part of the runway that connected with the lower level. For me, this only added to the thrill of the flight. Nevertheless, after a routine approach and somewhat bumpy landing, we taxied in toward the terminal greeted by machine-gun armed military guards stationed at the ends of the runway and all along leading back up to the terminal. Since the country had been engaged in a civil war for the past thirty-five years, visitors to Guatemala City had become accustomed to the presence of armed military all over the city.

One of the pilots on this flight happened to be the woman who was destined to become the captain of an aircraft involved in one of the most far-reaching aviation disasters in American history. While piloting a DC-9 on May 10, 1996, with 110 passengers on board, Captain Candalyn Kubeck took off from the Miami International Airport, bound for Atlanta. A few moments after takeoff, while climbing out, ValuJet flight #592 was engulfed in flames, and seconds later plunged into the Florida Everglades in a catastrophic crash killing all 110 people on board. The cause of the crash was later determined to be due to the explosion of several oxygen canisters which were in the forward cargo compartment. The controls of the aircraft were immediately destroyed, leaving the pilots unable to control the big jet.

Captain Kubeck nevertheless distinguished herself by becoming an airline captain in a profession long dominated by men. It seems that it was her destiny to be involved in the crash which resulted in tougher restrictions being placed on the aviation industry, particularly the no-frills airlines, which are so prevalent today.

You have probably heard the following riddle about the crash of the aircraft where there were only two survivors. Everyone was killed except the captain and a young male passenger. They were taken to different hospitals. The young passenger was the captain's son, but the captain was not his father. How could this be? It appears to be an unsolvable riddle, doesn't it? The answer is, of course, that the captain was a woman.

This story serves to point out the cultural gender

bias with regard to pilots. The pilot is female, but we assume she is male. Unfortunately, the same bias exists today in the workplace where discriminatory hiring practices still exist against women. Sexual discrimination in the workplace is rampant. Sexual discrimination seems to be standard operating procedure in many corporations in America and throughout the world as women continue to receive lower salaries for performing the same work as their male counterparts. Gender bias is a fact of life as more and more women enter the work force and seek to be rewarded for their efforts with promotions and salaries equal to men.

    Whenever I think of Guatemala, I can always see the eyes of the Mayan Indian mothers and their "little barefoot beggars" (as they are called) who always greeted us outside the terminal after our arrival. They had bracelets and beads for sale. They were barefoot with hardly any clothes on their backs, and they were there night after night to greet every incoming flight in hopes of making a few dollars to buy food. They absolutely broke our hearts as they followed us into the hotel begging for money and trying to sell us one more piece of jewelry. We always gave them a few dollars and returned home many times with their handmade bracelets, but it never seemed like we were doing enough. Their plight was due, in large part, to the oppression of the military regime brought about by decades of civil war and by politicians who were much more interested in accumulating their own fortunes than they were in caring for the parents and children on the streets of Guatemala City. Most of them were women who did not have husbands and the children did not have fathers to care for them, so they were left to their own devices of weaving their little bracelets and selling them at the airport night after night.

Too many of our churches seem to be sending young girls and women the message that it is only the men (deacons, elders, ministers, priests, etc.) who have access to the Spirit because it is only the men who have leadership positions in the church. My question is this: If over half of the people in the world are women, why would we want to limit the work of spreading and preaching the Gospel of Christ to less than half of the population? Why not use <u>all</u> God's people to do <u>all</u> God's work?

I have come to believe that the church's attitude and treatment of women over the centuries has contributed greatly to the second-class citizen status of women today. When young boys and girls and young men and women grow up and see their churches with their male leaders, priests, pastors, elders, deacons, bishops, teachers, communion servers, etc. placing restrictions on women in the church by not allowing them to be ordained to these same positions, I believe it plants in their minds the idea that women are fundamentally inferior to men. And remember, the churches are composed of women and men, and both women and men have allowed this discrimination to take place. When a young boy or young man is taught this at a very early age, it is extremely difficult to ever change that viewpoint as he matures into adulthood and assumes a position of leadership and responsibility within the church, the community, and the workplace. Even more importantly, we see this attitude within the family with more and more men abusing their wives, not treating them as equal partners in the marriage, and seeking to control them. Women, too, need to recognize this gender bias and not allow it to occur. (It really should come as no surprise to us that women have such an uphill battle in our society to gain equality when we look at the treatment of women in many churches.) I realize this bias is not true for all churches. However, in the vast majority of churches women simply do not have the same status as men. They are not afforded the same opportunities to be in the ministry. They are not encouraged to develop themselves into leadership roles without being subservient to a male pastor, minister, or priest. However, when we look at church roles, we see that, paradoxically, most of the members are women. Most of the work done in our churches is done by women. They are the ones bringing their children to church. Most of the nurturing, the praying, and caring for children is done by women. On any given Sunday morning, a far greater percentage of mothers are present in the pews of the congregations in this country than are fathers. A large portion of the men have deserted their families and are nowhere to be found or are "deadbeat dads" who do not support the mother and their children. Many men are simply not willing to make the commitment to become involved in the spiritual lives of their families. They seem to be much more interested in either sleeping late, reading the Sunday paper and getting ready for an afternoon filled with football, or playing golf, going fishing, or some other "guy thing." Many men apparently don't think it is "cool" to be involved in the church. Therefore, the responsibility for the children's spiritual development is by and large left in the mother's hands.

As more and more men have abdicated their positions of spiritual leadership alongside their wives, we see that families are in a greater state of crisis today than ever before in our history. Somehow men have gotten the message from our culture that men and women are not equal and that men are to be in positions of power and authority in the community while women are to be responsible for cooking, house cleaning, and taking the kids to Sunday School and church. These are indeed very important jobs, but women should be able to choose what they do without the fear of a "glass ceiling." I believe the genesis of this whole problem is the church and the restrictions placed on women in the vast majority of our churches. It is little wonder that doctors' offices are filled with far more women than men suffering from low self-esteem, depression, and anxiety. What else could the result be when young girls and young women are taught from an early age that they are not equal to boys and young men because there are so many things men can do in the church which women are not allowed to do? This entire problem can be traced to legalism and the use of isolated verses in the Bible out of context.

The Bible says in Genesis 1:27: "*So God created human beings, making them to be like himself. He created them male and female...*" (TEV) I understand this to mean that God considers men and women to be totally and completely equal in every way and that one is not to dominate the other, ever. Paul writes in Galatians 3:28 that men and women are equal in the sight of Jesus Christ. I take that to mean exactly what it says: that Jesus loves women and men equally in every way and that he places no restrictions on what either can do. Just look at the ministry of Jesus—everywhere he went he was surrounded by women who were faithful to Him, who were doing important work for him. When he died, who was the first person to see that he had arisen from the dead? It was **Mary Magdalene**. It is also obvious when reading the passages where Jesus talks about his mother, **Mary**, that he had a very tender and loving affection for her. Remember what Mary's reaction was when she was told by the angel, Gabriel, that the Holy Spirit had conceived Jesus within her womb? Her response was, *"I am the Lord's servant."* (Luke 1:38) She went to see her cousin **Elizabeth**. When Elizabeth opened the door to her home and heard Mary's voice, the baby *"leaped in her womb and Elizabeth was filled with the Holy Spirit."* (Luke 1:41) Mary then said: *My soul glorifies the Lord and my spirit rejoices in God my Savior, for he has been mindful of the humble state of this servant. From now on, all generations will call me blessed, for the mighty one has done great things for me. Holy is his name!* (Luke 1:46-49)

Mary was so grateful to God for what he had done for her that all she could think to do was magnify his name and praise him. It certainly sounds like God chose a woman for a vital role, doesn't it?

In the Old Testament, we find many examples of women whom God used in important ways. **Miriam** (Moses' sister) was a prophet and led the dancing at the Red Sea during the great exodus from Egypt (Ex 15:20). In II Kings 22, we find the account of the prophet, **Hulda**, as she interpreted the Book of the Law for the Israelites. **Deborah** was a prophet who led Israel to victory over the Canaanites (Jdg 4-5).

Esther was chosen by God to be a queen (Est 2), and distinguished herself in God's service and is one of the most revered figures in the Old Testament to this day.

Look at the account of the boy Jesus at the temple in Luke, chapter 2. After Jesus left his parents and had been gone for three days, they finally found him sitting in the temple with the teachers, listening to them and asking them questions:

Mary said, "Son, why have you treated us like this? Your father and I have been anxiously searching for you." "Why were you searching for me?" he asked. "Didn't you know I had to be in my father's house?" But they did not understand what he was saying to them, so then he went down to Nazareth with them and was obedient to them. But his mother treasured all these things in her heart. And Jesus grew in wisdom and stature and in favor with God and men." (Luke 2:48-52)

What mother can't identify with the feelings of Mary in this instance? Who of us would be where we are today but for the love of a mother or someone who provided a mother's love?

On the day when he was crucified, Jesus' mother and a group of other women were there at the foot of the cross to be with him in his moment of greatest need. We are not told where Joseph was or if the disciples were there. In John 19:25-27 we read:

Near the cross of Jesus stood his mother; his mother's sister; **Mary**, *the wife of Clopas; and Mary Magdalene. When Jesus saw his mother there and* *the disciple whom he loved (John) standing nearby, he said to his mother, "Dear woman, here is your son," and to the disciple, "Here is your mother."*

From that time on, the disciple, John, took her into his home. Forty days after his resurrection, as Jesus was ascending into heaven, there was Mary again. In Acts 1:14 we read, *"They all joined together constantly, along with the women and Mary, the mother of Jesus, and with his brothers."* There she was, with him right to the end, loving him, supporting him, praying for him, all the way. Her faithfulness and motherly love are wonderful examples for everyone. Jesus' mother, Mary, however, was not the only woman who had an important part in Jesus' life. Look at the account of Jesus in the home of **Martha** and her sister **Mary**. Martha was busy working while her sister Mary sat at the Lord's feet listening intently to what he had to say. When Martha complained, Jesus answered her, *"You are worried and upset about many things, but only one thing is needed. Mary has chosen what is better and it will not be taken away from her."* (Luke 10:41-42) Later on, while Jesus was at Bethany on his way to Jerusalem to be crucified, it was Martha who served dinner to Jesus while Mary anointed him with expensive perfume. As the Bible tells us in John 12:3, *"Mary poured the perfume on Jesus' feet and wiped his feet with her hair and the house was filled with the fragrance of the perfume."* Earlier, when Lazarus, the brother of Martha and Mary died and Mary had come to the Lord in tears, we read, *" When Jesus saw her weeping and the Jews who had come along with her also weeping, He was deeply moved in spirit and trou-*

bled. Where have you laid him?" He asked. "Come and see Lord," they replied. "Jesus wept." (John 11:33-35) Jesus was so deeply moved at the death of Lazarus and the grieving of Martha and Mary that he raised Lazarus from the dead in one of the most dramatic miracles in the New Testament.

Mary Magdalene was another woman who loved the Lord and who was helpful to him in his ministry. In Luke, chapter 8, we read:

"After this Jesus traveled about from one town and village to another proclaiming the good news of the kingdom of God. The Twelve were with him and also some women who had been cured of some evil spirits and diseases: Mary, called Magdalene, from whom seven demons had come out; **Joanna***, the wife of Cuza, the manager of Herod's household;* **Susanna** *and many others. These women were helping to support them out of their own means."*

In other words, they were giving Jesus time and money to promote his ministry in one of the first examples of Christian charity we know of. Mary Magdalene, we know, was standing right beside Jesus' mother, Mary, at the foot of the cross at the moment of his death and when Jesus was buried, Mary Magdalene and Jesus' mother were *"sitting there opposite the tomb."* (Matthew 27:61) When the angel appeared and rolled back the stone to the tomb, he told the two women that Jesus was not dead, but had arisen. Mary Magdalene and Mary then went inside the tomb and saw the empty shroud. They ran to tell his disciples and according to Matthew 28:9:

Suddenly Jesus met them. "Greetings," he said. They came to him, clasped his feet and worshipped him. Then Jesus said to them, "Do not be afraid. Go and tell my brothers to go to Galilee. There they will see me."

Jesus had the utmost confidence in these women and gave them the job of making sure that all of the other followers found out about his resurrection. Again, quite an important job, don't you think?

The prophet, **Anna**, is another woman who appears in the New Testament in an important role. Anna was the daughter of Phanuel and was 84 years old, having been a widow for many years. The Bible says that she never left the temple, but that she worshipped night and day, fasting and praying. When Jesus was being presented at the temple, Anna saw him coming up to the temple with his mother and father and as the Bible says, *"At that very moment she gave thanks to God and spoke about the child to all who were looking forward to the redemption of Jerusalem"* (Luke 2:38). In the 21st chapter of Acts we read the story of Phillip, the evangelist, who was one of the Seven (the first deacons of the Jerusalem church) sent out to tell the good news. Phillip had four unmarried daughters who were also prophets. In Romans 16, Paul writes in verses 1 and 2:

*"I commend to you our sister **Phoebe**, a servant (deacon) of the church in Cenchrea. I ask you to receive her in the Lord in a way worthy of the saints and to give her any help she may need from you, for*

she has been a great help to many people including me."

Phoebe had been serving as a deacon in the church there at East Corinth and apparently had been a tremendous blessing to Paul and all the brothers and sisters. Paul goes on to say in verse 3, *"Greet **Priscilla** and Aquila, my fellow workers in Christ Jesus. They risked their lives for me, not only I but all the churches of the Gentiles are grateful to them."* Priscilla and her husband Aquila had accompanied Paul when he sailed from Corinth to Syria. Paul had left them in Ephesus to continue preaching the good news there where they subsequently met Apollos, a native of Alexandria. He was an educated man with a thorough knowledge of the Scriptures. It was in Ephesus that Apollos was taught more deeply the message of the Gospel of Christ by Priscilla and Aquila. Later, Paul writes in I Co 16:19, *"The churches in the province of Asia send you greetings. Aquila and Priscilla greet you warmly in the Lord and so does the church that meets at their house."* Apparently, Priscilla and Aquila had been co-pastoring the home church which was meeting in their house.

In I Co 11:5, Paul, the apostle, acknowledges that women pray and prophesy in the church. We know that after Paul and Silas had been released from prison that the first place they went was to **Lydia**'s house. In I Tim 3:11, where Paul is giving instructions to Timothy about pastors and deacons, the following verse has been incorrectly translated in many modern translations of the Bible: *"In the same way, **their wives** are to be women worthy of respect, not mali-*

cious talkers but temperate and trustworthy in everything." The Greek word for "their wives" refers to the female deacons who served the church. The meaning intended by the original author has been lost, unfortunately, by the (predominantly male) translators.

There are many other examples in the New Testament of women being used by the Holy Spirit to help the ministry of Jesus. Many, many women had important roles in the first century church. Jesus placed no restrictions on women. On the contrary, he was surrounded by women throughout all of his ministry and obviously held them in equal esteem with the men who followed him. **The point is, Jesus did not discriminate against women either in the church or outside the church and neither should we.**

Remember, at Pentecost when the Holy Spirit came, both **men and women** received the anointing and power of God's Spirit. *"Even on my servants, both men and women, I will pour out my Spirit in those days, and they will prophesy." (Acts 2:18)* It is clear that God has given to women the same blessing and responsibility of ministry which he has given to men!

Many of the most spirit-filled people in the world today are women. Amy Grant, the Christian and pop singer, has spent her entire career singing about her faith in Christ and her personal relationship with her Savior. As a Christian singer who has crossed over to the pop genre, she has had a tremendous influence as a role model for young women.

Former Miss America, Heather Whitestone, the first hearing-impaired contestant to win that title, did an interpretive dance to the Christian song, <u>Via Dolorosa</u>, in the talent portion of the contest. Upon winning the title of Miss America, she was quick to give credit to the Lord and to thank Him for all of her blessings.

Another former Miss America, Teri Meeuwsen, co-host of the 700 Club on the Family Channel, has become a fine example of what a spirit-filled woman can accomplish on television. Likewise, Kathie Lee Gifford, former co-host of the Regis and Kathie Lee show, has produced an annual Christmas special for television in which the focus of the program is on Jesus Christ as the reason for the season.

Mother Theresa of Calcutta was an obvious spirit-filled woman who made her mark in the twentieth century. She was perhaps the most admired and best known person (man or woman) in the world and was a Nobel laureate. Her work in the poorest part of Calcutta and her ministry to the "untouchables" there, those whom few others would care for, made her a spiritual giant in the world's eye. She was quoted as saying that the poorest of the poor there in Calcutta do not die from lack of food or medical attention but they do die from the feeling that no one cares for them.

Ruth Graham, the wife of evangelist Billy Graham, has emerged in the latter years of his ministry as the real spiritual leader of the family, having raised six children virtually by herself while Billy was off evangelizing publicly in various countries around the world. (Billy has spoken of his regret for not having spent more time with his children while they were growing up). Ruth's spiritual leadership and support of her husband's entire ministry has now become well known and she has had a tremendous ministry in her own right.

Catherine Marshall, the late wife of the former

U.S. Senate Chaplain, Peter Marshall, after his death became a best-selling Christian author. Her book on the Holy Spirit, The Helper, has sold millions of copies in several different languages around the world and has helped millions upon millions of believers to become filled with the Holy Spirit and put his power to work in their lives. She also wrote Christy, which was turned into a television series about a woman who devoted herself to Christian work with landlocked people in the Appalachian Mountains.

Helen Sherrill, the author of Christian Parenting and a dear friend to my family and me, was one of the most important people in my spiritual journey. The peace and serenity which she exuded along with the deep spiritual wisdom which she spoke made a lasting impression on me at a time when I was just beginning to feel God moving in my life and my children were still toddlers.

I believe that I am a Christian today, devoted to God in large part, because of the unceasing prayers of my own mother for me. Her faith in Christ and constant intercession on my behalf seem far more important to me today than when I was growing up. How fortunate is the child who has Christian parents praying for her or him night and day throughout their lives.

After all these years I can still see the eyes of those Mayan women on the street outside the airport in Guatemala City who were there for the purpose of making enough money to feed their children. It is the spiritual food and nourishment with which women are uniquely endowed and are able to give to their children and others in addition to food for sustenance, which is a "pearl of great value" to all of us.

Spiritual Jetstreams

Chapter 3

How To Be Filled With The Spirit

Therefore, I urge you, brothers, in view of God's mercy, to offer your bodies as living sacrifices, holy and pleasing to God—this is your spiritual act of worship. Do not conform any longer to the pattern of this world, but be transformed by the renewing of your mind. Then you will be able to test and approve what God's will is—his good, pleasing and perfect will. For by the grace given me I say to every one of you: Do not think of yourself more highly than you ought, but rather think of yourself with sober judgment, in accordance with the measure of faith God has given you. Just as each of us has one body with many members, and these members do not all have the same function, so in Christ we who are many form one body, and each member belongs to all the others. We have different gifts, according to the grace given us. If a man's gift is prophesying, let him use it in proportion to his faith. If it is serving, let him serve, if it is teaching, let him teach; if it is encouraging, let him encourage, if it is contributing to the needs of others, let him give generously; if it is leadership, let him govern diligently; if it is showing mercy, let him do it cheerfully.
(Romans 12:1-8 NIV)

"...be transformed by the renewing of your mind."
(Romans 12:2b)

"Today our flight from Miami to Cali, Colombia, will take us down over Cuba where you'll be able to see the Bay of Pigs just off the right side of the aircraft as we pass over the southern coast of Cuba and out over the Caribbean. Next you'll see Grand Cayman Island and then the Blue Mountains of Jamaica before heading out over open waters. As we approach South America, we will pass just west of Baranquilla, Colombia and Cartagena will be off to the right. The 19,000' permanently snow-capped twin peaks of Mount Simon Bolivar and Mount Cristobal Colon will be visible off the left wing. They are part of the Sierra Nevada da Santa Marta Mountain range, which is the highest coastal mountain range in the world. We'll then enter the Andes and overfly Medellin before beginning our descent for landing into the Cali airport. This is some of the most spectacular scenery you'll ever see. We'll be cruising at an altitude of 37,000' at a speed of Mach .84 (about 550 mph) and our trip today should take us approximately 3 1/2 hours."

As I made this announcement from the flight deck of our Boeing 727, it struck me that most of us go through life at a break-neck speed without ever stopping to slow down our frenetic lifestyles. We may not be traveling at Mach .84, but we are surely going at a pace that God never intended when he created us. We have become the "short attention span generation" in our futile quest to do more, spend more, have more, and keep more than any generation in history.

It is no wonder that ours has been called the "age of anxiety" as doctor's offices and hospitals are filled to overflowing with men, women, boys, and girls suffering from anxiety-related complaints ranging from eating disorders and panic attacks to headaches and severe depression. A new generation of women has emerged called "Soccer Moms" who have too much to do with too little time and help to do it. Drug abuse and alcoholism are at all-time highs, our prisons are overflowing, child abuse and teenage pregnancies are rising, and we have placed our faith in political leaders from both parties who seem to have no concept of truth and integrity as their re-election campaigns are financed by special interest groups (political action committees) who gladly give millions to promote their own agendas. These leaders can hardly be expected to make unbiased decisions which are in the best interests of the American people when they are so financially obligated to their "benefactors."

Yet, we have apparently learned nothing from the past as we continue to look for **secular solutions to spiritual problems**. We are still seeking social and economic solutions to all the problems which plague our so-called "enlightened society." Federal judges at every level continue to wield extreme power over our lives as they rule time and again to throw out conventional wisdom and the will of the people in favor of unprecedented decisions favoring secular humanism over what once was considered common decency. For example, a federal judge in New York recently ruled that a teenager who brought a gun to school and was suspended had his civil rights violated by the teachers who took the gun from him. In another state, a federal judge ruled in favor of same-sex marriages (in direct conflict with God's moral law-Ro 1:26-27), while the Supreme Court has thrown God's Ten Commandments out of the public schools. Whatever happened to "...one nation, under God?"

It does not really take a NASA rocket scientist to figure out that our country is in a spiritual crisis. We have produced, in the past two generations, a population of biblical and spiritual illiterates. We are suffering from "spiritual malnutrition" as we continue to raise up millions and millions of children who have little or no parental involvement in their spiritual maturation and development. The result is, of course, that the overwhelming majority of today's young people have no knowledge of God's word (the Bible!), no faith in Jesus Christ as their personal Savior, and no clue about who the Holy Spirit is. The unique concept of personal responsibility has been all but forgotten and has been replaced by the humanistic mantra, "If it makes me feel good, then I'll do it!"

If ours really is a spiritual problem (and I'm convinced that it is), then it follows that the only way to solve it is through a spiritual solution. In Romans 12, the apostle Paul writes that we should stop conforming to the pattern of popular culture and "...be transformed by the renewing of (our) minds." It is interesting to note that the word Paul used for "**transformed**" is the same word from which we derive the word "**metamorphosis**." It's the process by which a caterpillar becomes a beautiful butterfly. In the same way, we are to be transformed (or metamorphosed) into a higher order, a completely new being, and the process must begin in our thought life (which is really where we all live). We must seek to renew our minds through spiritual disciplines such as daily Bible study, meditating on God's word, and spending time in regular prayer with the Lord. We need to slow down and allow time for

God's Spirit to speak to our spirits so that we can understand what his good and perfect will is for our lives. With our short attention spans which characterize "Generation X" we want instant if not lasting solutions. Unfortunately, God simply doesn't work that way. There are no shortcuts to true spirituality and we must make a regular investment of time spent in the presence of the Lord if we are to grow to spiritual maturity.

Wisdom from the Spirit is explained in I Corinthians 2:

God has revealed his wisdom to us by his Spirit who searches all things, even the deep things of God...We have received the Spirit of God so that we may understand what God has freely given us. We speak in words taught by the Spirit, expressing spiritual truths in spiritual words. People without the Spirit do not accept the things that come from the Spirit of God because they are spiritually discerned and they don't understand them and think they are foolish. But we have the mind of Christ.

Our dilemma is really **spiritual warfare**. Like Paul, we don't understand the things we do. Instead of doing the things which we know to be right, we tend to do the exact opposite because of our sinful nature within us waging war against our minds and spirits. (Romans 7) Fortunately, God has a solution for our dilemma in Ephesians 5:

Be filled with the Spirit.

This imperative is written in the present tense which means a continuous filling throughout our lives as we grow spiritually. If we live by the Spirit, we will not always be trying to satisfy the desires of our human natures (if it feels good, do it!). Our human nature is contrary to the Spirit and they are in conflict with each other. The consequence is that we find it impossible to successfully do and say the things we really want. It is only by yielding our stubbornness and surrendering to the Spirit of Christ that we make it possible for him to produce his fruit in our lives. *The fruit of the Spirit is love, joy, peace, patience, kindness, goodness, faithfulness, gentleness, and self-control.* (Galatians 5:23) It is precisely at this point that most of us run into a problem. We want, most of all, to feel like we're in control of our lives and that if we work hard and make enough money and try to be good and successful according to today's standards, then we will please God and be admired and respected by our friends, family, and the world we live in. For most of us, it is ludicrous to even consider yielding complete control of our lives to the Holy Spirit because it would mean that we are not in control. The truth is, we are not really in control anyway, but to admit such a thing strikes at the very heart of our pride and makes us appear weak and simple-minded to most of those whom we come in contact with every day.

    Consider this fact: According to the Bible, there are two persons praying for you at this very moment. *Jesus is at the right hand of God and is also interceding (praying) for us.* (Romans 8:34)

    In the same way the Spirit helps us in our weak-

ness. We do not know what we ought to pray for, but the Spirit himself intercedes (prays) for us with sighs that words cannot express. (Romans 8:26-27)
That's right, even though you may not be aware of it, Jesus and the Holy Spirit are praying for you right now and interceding on your behalf. Jesus promised that the Holy Spirit, our Helper and Comforter, would be with us always. (John 14) In II Corinthians 3, Paul wrote:

The Spirit of the living God written on human hearts the Lord is the Spirit and where the Spirit of the Lord is,
there is freedom. And we all reflect the Lord's glory and are being transformed (metamorphosed) into his likeness with
ever-increasing glory, which comes from the Lord, who is the Spirit.

In Phillipians 1:19, we read, "...*the help given (to me) by the Spirit of Jesus.*" The Holy Spirit is called "**the Spirit of Jesus**" and that's exactly who he is. I like to think of the Holy Spirit as "God the Father and Jesus at work in the world." I've found this to be a great help to me in understanding who the Holy Spirit is and what he does. He's not some mystical ghost floating around like Casper, but he's real and present here and he wants to help us to fulfill God's plan for our lives. The key is, we have to be willing to let him help us and we must invite him into our hearts so that he can do his work in us. The Holy Spirit wants to transform us into a new creation just like the butterfly.
In the movie, *Mr. Holland's Opus*, Richard

Dreyfuss plays a high school music teacher. In it, he is reflecting on his life and tells a friend that he has changed his behavior from when he was a young man and that he no longer does the things he used to, things that he is ashamed of now because they were wrong and are now repugnant to him. He says, "I'm different now. I'm not the man I used to be." When we ask the Holy Spirit to come into our hearts and make us a new creation, he will so drastically alter who we are that the old self is practically indiscernable anymore. We become totally and completely different from the person we used to be just as the butterfly no longer looks or acts anything like a caterpillar. Our family and friends and the people we work with will recognize that a radical change has taken place and will immediately know that something has happened as the Holy Spirit begins to influence every area of our lives. If we will ask the Holy Spirit to come into our lives, then we will develop a thirst for God's word that will only be satisfied by spending time in **Bible reading, prayer,** and **meditation**.

The word "**Christophobic**" has become part of our modern vocabulary as we see more and more signs of an increasingly liberal and secular society turning its back on God. The word literally means "fear of Christ" and is used to characterize those who seek to remove all reference to God and Jesus from every aspect of society.

I want to suggest a new word be added to our vocabulary. The word is "**Charisphobic**." That is, the fear of the Holy Spirit and the gifts of the Holy Spirit. I believe that we are living in what has come to be known as the "post-Christian era" due to the total neglect of the Holy Spirit and his place in our lives. Even among most self-professing Christians, there is a fear of yielding or surrendering to the Holy Spirit because of what he might ask us to do. Most people don't want to make a real commitment to let the Holy Spirit be in control because they are afraid he might ask them to give up some of their material possessions and begin to live a life of service. Service to the Lord and to his children should be the top priority for all believers. But, sadly, service usually is in last place when we start talking about the things most important to us. Accumulating possessions, power, and entertaining ourselves are far more important to the vast majority of people. The **pursuit of pleasure** has become the top priority as men and women spend every waking moment trying to find satisfaction and meaning for their lives while looking in all the wrong places. Charisphobia rules the day as society seemingly goes to any length to avoid making a spiritual commitment to do God's will. People are afraid that they will have to give up some of their precious possessions or pursuits if they come under the power of the Holy Spirit.

    Francis Schaeffer, the Christian author and founder of the L'Abri spiritual retreat in Switzerland, said that we should all try to mature to the point where our lives would be characterized by "**moment-by-moment true spirituality**." That is, we would act at any given moment on the beliefs which we say we have as Christians. Not part of the time or most of the time, but all of the time.

    Let me simply encourage you to begin today, right where you are, right now to spend some time in the presence of the Holy Spirit. Just close your eyes and say "bon jour Holy Spirit," "guten morgen Holy Spirit," "buenos dias Holy Spirit," "**good morning Holy Spirit**," or whatever you're comfortable with. Ask the Spirit to come into your heart and mind and be your helper and friend from this day on for the rest of your life. Feel the presence of Jesus' Spirit as you breathe in (it's alright to inhale!) and the release of worries and frustrations as you exhale. Turn your palms up to Heaven as you submit to God's Spirit and receive a fresh infilling of peace and light as your anxieties fade away. Ask the Spirit to help you pray to the Father and you'll find that you can pray just as naturally as if you were talking to a close friend. Ask the Spirit to help you with any problem you're having and you'll see why he's called the "Helper." I often find that if I'm having a particularly hard time dealing with a situation in my life, that if I just ask the Holy Spirit to take care of this problem for me today and carry it for me for awhile, I'll get immediate relief and respite from it. That which seemed so overwhelming to me just a few minutes ago is now something I can manage and successfully deal with.

    Let me remind you that when you pray to or speak with the Holy Spirit you're really speaking to Jesus and the Father as well. When you're praying to your Heavenly Father you're doing so through the Spirit. When you call on Jesus it's the Spirit of Jesus who is within you who speaks on your behalf. The Holy Spirit really is "God the Father and Jesus at work in the world." You don't need to be afraid of the Spirit or what you might be asked to do as the "Charisphobics" and "Christophobics" are. On the contrary, you can welcome him into your life and take advantage of everything he wants to do for you as the best friend you'll ever have. All you have to do is **ASK**. Stop living at Mach .84 and start living at **God Speed** instead. You'll get more done, be better rested, and you'll safely arrive at the destination that God intends for you.

Sit back...Relax...Enjoy the trip! And thanks for flying with us.

David Huddleston

Spiritual Jetstreams

Chapter 4

Slipping Through The Spiritual Jetstream

Therefore, there is now no condemnation for those who are in Christ Jesus, because through Christ Jesus the law of the Spirit of life set me free from the law of sin and death. For what the law was powerless to do in that it was weakened by the sinful nature, God did by sending his own Son in the likeness of sinful man to be a sin offering. And so he condemned sin in sinful man, in order that the righteous requirements of the law might be fully met in us, who do not live according to the sinful nature but according to the Spirit.

Those who live according to the sinful nature have their minds set on what that nature desires, but those who live in accordance with the Spirit have their minds set on what the Spirit desires. The mind of sinful man is death, but the mind controlled by the Spirit is life and peace; The sinful mind is hostile to God. It does not submit to God's law, nor can it do so. Those controlled by the sinful nature cannot please God.

You, however, are controlled not by the sinful nature but by the Spirit, if the Spirit of God Lives in you. And if anyone does not have the Spirit of Christ, he does not belong to Christ. But if Christ is in you, your body is dead because of sin, yet your spirit is alive because of righteousness. And if the Spirit of him who raised Jesus from the dead is living in you, he who raised Christ from the dead will also give life to your mortal bodies through his Spirit, who lives in you.

Therefore, brothers, we have an obligation--but it is not to the sinful nature, to live according to it. For if you live according to the sinful nature, you will die; but if by the Spirit you put to death the misdeeds of the body, you will live, because those who are led by the Spirit of God are sons of God. For you did not receive a spirit that makes you a slave again to fear, but you received the Spirit of sonship. And by him we cry, "Abba, Father." The Spirit himself testifies with our spirit that we are God's children. Now if we are children, then we are heirs--heirs of God and co-heirs with Christ, if indeed we share in his sufferings in order that we may also share in his glory.
(Romans 8:1-17)

"...those who are led by the Spirit of God are sons (and daughters) of God."
(Romans 8:14)

"Eastern 296, you're flying 'ELB' tonight, aren't you?" crackled the Washington Center air traffic controller as we clipped along at a ground speed of 700 miles per hour. "ELB" (ears laid back) was his way of saying that we were traveling at a higher than normal speed, in a canine reference to our most excellent ground speed. We had departed Hartsfield International Airport in Atlanta (ATL) on a bitterly cold February night enroute to Newark International Airport which serves the New York area. A fast-moving cold front was approaching from the southwest due to the prevailing jet stream location which wound around like a snake from the Pacific northwest down through Texas, Louisiana, Mississippi, and Alabama before heading up through Georgia on its way to New England. After takeoff on runway 9 left, we turned northeast to a heading of 040° as we began our climb to the assigned altitude of 37,000'. After passing through 18,000' MSL (mean sea level) we reset our altimeters to 29.92 (inches of mercury, also known as "pressure altitude") and began to notice that our ground speed far exceeded our true air speed which indicated the presence of a strong tail wind. This is every pilot's dream since it means you might actually save some time enroute and arrive at your destination ahead of schedule.

As we finally leveled off at flight level 370 (37,000') and got up to normal cruise speed of 550 mph we saw that our ground speed indicator was reading 700 mph! This meant that we had slipped into the jetstream and had a tailwind of 150 mph helping us along toward our destination of EWR (Newark). Fantastic! We were proceeding through the night skies ELB! Watch out, New York, here we come! The OAT (outside air temperature) was -50 C and we were cutting a blue streak through air! The jetstream was helping us along every minute of the way.

Just think what a help it would be to us if we had someone to give us a boost and help us along the way as we live our lives. Someone who would care for us and be our best friend and constant companion. Someone who would always be there when we need counsel and answers to life's questions. Before I started flying big jets, I was a flight instructor teaching students to fly in a small Cessna 150 two-seater. I had to be very careful to prepare my students thoroughly before turning them loose for their first solo flight. I had to make sure all their questions were answered and they had received all the guidance I could possibly give them prior to getting out of the aircraft and watching them taxi out alone to perform the three "touch-and-go" landings necessary to solo (usually in the presence of their families!).

The truth is, this person is already available to us and is just waiting for us to invite him in so he can take up permanent residence within us. He's known by various names. Some call him the **Helper**. To others he's known as the **Counselor**. Still others call him the **Comforter**. Regardless of what you call him, he's really the **Holy Spirit** and above all else he wants to be the closest friend you'll ever have because he loves you in spite of all your faults. He cares for you in a way you can't understand in spite of all the things you've done in the past which you may regret or be ashamed of. He wants to help you, counsel you, comfort you, and show you a better way of living, but only if you desire his company. Like any good friend, he will not enter into your own life unless he is invited.

The miracle is that all you have to do in order to enjoy all he has to offer is this: **Simply invite him in!** Ask the Holy Spirit to come into your heart through faith in Christ, and he will. Ask him to take control of your life and take charge of every area, and he will be more than happy to. You'll find that his presence in you will bring you a new security that you have never experienced before. In every situation, he'll be there to comfort you when you need comforting. He'll lead you to make wise and correct decisions as he counsels you about every area of your life.

Whether it's your relationship with your husband, wife, boyfriend, girlfriend, friends, family, the people you work with, a personal problem you've encountered, or whatever the situation, the Spirit will always be there to help you along and make your way a little easier as he works in your life to make you the very best you can be.

Jesus said in John 14:15-16, "I will ask the Father and he will give you another Counselor (Comforter or Helper) to be with you forever, the Spirit of truth who lives with you and will be in you." **I like to think of the Holy Spirit as God the Father and Jesus the Son at work in the world.** Jesus asked his Father to give us another Helper (besides himself) to come and live in us forever to be our comforter and friend. And his Father honored his request. All we have to do is ask him to come and take up residence in our hearts, and he will be faithful to do just that as he helps us to start "slipping through the Spiritual jetstream." As the apostle Paul said in Romans 8:14-16,

"...those who are led by the Spirit of God are sons *(and daughters)* of God. For you did not receive a spirit that makes you a slave again to fear, but you received the Spirit of sonship. And by him we cry, 'Abba, Father.' The Spirit himself testifies with our spirit that we are God's children."

If we will only let the Spirit of God lead us we will never again be "slaves to fear" and God will always consider us to be his children. He will help and encourage us and will give us the courage to live our lives as people of integrity. We will have no fear of being pressured into compromising our values just because popular culture tells us we are wrong and foolish to put our trust in a poor carpenter who lived 2000 years ago. We will be able to go to our Father in confidence and talk to him through the Holy Spirit with the full knowledge that he hears us and cares for us with love and understanding that will help us through every stage of life.

That jetstream I got into on my flight from ATL to EWR was a big help to me and it was one of the coolest things ever to be doing 700 mph over the earth. But, it was nothing by comparison to God's Spiritual jetstream. That jetstream between ATL and EWR was temporary, but God's Spiritual jetstream is always available to help us. And the most awesome thing is that it's always blowing in just the right direction to give us the maximum help to get us where the Lord wants us to be. Just ask the Spirit of God to find a home within you. Before you know it you, too, will be slipping along "ELB" in the Spiritual jetstream!

Have a nice flight!

Spiritual Jetstreams

Chapter 5

Trusting The Spirit Of Jesus

"Do not let your hearts be troubled. Trust in God: trust also in me. In my Father's house are many rooms; if it were not so, I would have told you. I am going there to prepare a place for you. And if I go and prepare a place for you, I will come back and take you to be with me that you also may be where I am. You know the way to the place where I am going."

Thomas said to him, "Lord, we don't know where you are going, so how can we know the way?"

Jesus answered, "I am the way and the truth and the life. No one comes to the Father except through me. If you really knew me, you would know my Father as well. From now on, you do know him and have seen him.

Philip said, "Lord, show us the Father and that will be enough for us."

Jesus answered: "Don't you know me, Philip, even after I have been among you such a long time? Anyone who has seen me has seen the Father. How can you say, 'Show us the Father'? Don't you believe that I am in the Father, and that the Father is in me?' The words I say to you are not just my own. Rather, it is the Father, living in me, who is doing his work. Believe me when I say that I am in the Father and the Father is in me; or at least believe on the evidence of

the miracles themselves. I tell you the truth, anyone who has faith in me will do what I have been doing. He will do even greater things than these, because I am going to the Father. And I will do whatever you ask in my name, so that the Son may bring glory to the Father. You may ask me for anything in my name, and I will do it."
(John 14:1-14)

"Trust in God; trust also in me....I am the way and the truth and the life. No one comes to the Father except through me."
(John14:1b, 6b)

When Coach Rick Pitino was preparing his University of Kentucky basketball team to play in the Final Four against the University of Massachusetts, he was asked by a New York sportswriter how he felt about the Wildcats' chances of winning the NCAA championship. Pitino responded, "We feel like we need to strike while the iron is hot (while we have all these great players on this year's team) in order to put ourselves in the best possible position to win the NCAA Final Four and bring this championship back to the people and the state of Kentucky." Kentucky had three players that year who would all become first-round NBA draft picks. Guard Tony Delk (Charlotte Hornets), forward Walter McCarty (New York Knicks), and swingman Antoine Walker (Boston Celtics) were all chosen in the first round just two months after leading their team to the national title. Two other starters, forward Ron Mercer (Boston Celtics) and center Mark Pope (Indianapolis Pacers), both joined the NBA the following year.

Frequently, on long flights, we would tune in top sporting events on our cockpit radio so we could keep track of some of our favorite teams while we were in the air. We would check on the scores briefly without interrupting air traffic control transmissions since our ADF (automatic direction finder) radio receiver was separate from our two main navigation and communication (nav/com) radios. Many airline pilots are also big sports fans and many are former athletes, as well. Like Pitino, pilots also want to put themselves (and their passengers) in the best possible position to succeed. Pitino does this by going all out to win the tournament when he has great players. Pilots do this by giving their passengers a safe, smooth flight to their destination. This involves putting your trust in your flight crew as well as your cabin crew, your aircraft and the ground crew which maintains it, and in the air traffic controllers who provide you with adequate vertical and horizontal separation from other aircraft. You must also learn to trust the controllers to guide you around severe weather while trusting your on-board weather radar to display accurate information. Everything involves **trust** at one level or another.

Pitino's words to "...strike while the iron is hot in order to put ourselves in the best possible position to win" proved to be prophetic. His team was hot, they struck, and they put themselves in the best possible position to win (after defeating U. Mass, two nights later U.K. won the NCAA with a relatively easy win over the Orangemen of Syracuse University).

What if you could find a way to put yourself in the best possible position to live a life which would bring happiness and victory? To live a life that would allow you to enjoy the fulfillment which you are so desperately seeking; a life that would provide the happiness and peace you want while enriching your relationships with your family and friends; a new way of living that would provide you with a deep spiritual understanding of your purpose in life and God's plan for you. (Yes, God does have a specific purpose for placing you on this earth!) The good news is that there is a way which God has provided for us to realize the happiness and personal fulfillment which we long for. We have been given the means to have a deep spiritual understanding of our purpose in life and the Lord's plan for us. **We must learn to trust the Spirit of**

Jesus to provide for our every need.

In the 14th chapter of John, Jesus speaks to his followers in a comforting tone. He is trying to show them a better way of living--a way of living that will bring honor to Jesus himself while finding favor in the eyes of his heavenly Father. He tells them not to be upset or discouraged, but to simply "*Trust in God and also in me.*" Thomas questioned him, "*Lord, we don't know where you are going, so how can we know the way?*" Jesus answered, "*I am the way and the truth and the life. No one comes to the Father except through me.*" (John 14:6)

According to Jesus, all you have to do is place your trust in him and that immediately puts you in the "best possible position" with your heavenly Father to receive his blessings on your life. He gives you these priceless blessings through his **Holy Spirit** working in your life. The Spirit goes with you everywhere to help you in every situation and in every emergency. He encourages you and takes care of your disappointments while he takes the hurts away and comforts you.

You must make a personal decision to trust Jesus and obey his teachings. The best way to find out what Jesus wants you to do is to spend some time each day reading the "owners manual" (also known as the Bible!). If we would all devote just a fraction of the time to our spiritual development that we do to our physical or intellectual development, it will pay great dividends in terms of the quality of our lives. Unfortunately, our spiritual development, which is by far the most critical and important to our well-being, is the area we probably spend the least amount of time on. We may have no qualms about spending hundreds or even thousands of hours every year on physical conditioning and development. We might gladly spend hundreds or even thousands of dollars yearly on health clubs, exercise equipment, diet centers, weight-loss medications, and personal trainers. We probably think nothing of investing many years and many thousands of dollars chasing degrees and knowledge in the belief that we will ultimately find happiness and security at the end of our academic rainbows. Yet, the mere mention of spending a few minutes each day reading and studying God's word as his Holy Spirit guides us along sounds ludicrous to most people. What a titanic waste of time! What good is it, we ask. How will it benefit me? Will it make me richer? Thinner? Smarter? Stronger? Better looking? Will I live longer and be healthier? Will I finally find my 15 minutes of fame? These are the typical responses most often heard when people are asked why they don't spend more time in Bible study or meditation and prayer. I don't have time, they say. But, will they have time to be miserable later on? Anxiety and depression are inevitably the result of **spiritual malnutrition**. They go hand-in-hand. If we don't exercise, we can expect to be physically unfit and out of shape. If we don't go to school and get an education, we can't expect to be in very good intellectual shape. Why, then, can we be surprised to find our personal lives are often an out-of-control mess when we haven't made any investment of time or energy in our spiritual development? None of us can grow to spiritual maturity automatically just because we are maturing chronologically. God just doesn't work that way because he knows it's not in our best interest to remain as **spiritual infants.**

    Madison Avenue and the entertainment industry have bombarded women and men with the message that in order to be happy and successful, we must be thin. Magazine covers, television shows, movies, and other entertainers all push the idea that you can't be too thin or too rich. What a lie and tremendous disservice to all of us! Self-image plummets, junior high peer pressure to be thin escalates (they're all dieting), and a life-long struggle with a healthy body image is born. The end result is **spiritual bankruptcy** as Satan, the enemy of our souls, uses low self-esteem to undermine our faith and trust in the Lord. After all, if we see ourselves as being unattractive or unlovable, how can God possibly love us? How could your boyfriend or husband or wife or girlfriend love you? What about co-workers, friends, or family? A vicious cycle is set up whereby the more we aspire to the standards of popular culture and society, the more unattainable they become because they are always changing. And, the more unattainable they become, the more we want to conform to them! This gives rise to an internal conflict within us which involves the way our body looks and the way we think it should look. This is precisely why many women and men are dissatisfied and unhappy with some aspect of their figures. While the plastic surgeons, health spas, and diet centers have enjoyed a windfall, today's women are particularly hostage to the "you can't be too thin" mentality and are paying a horrific ransom in terms of poor self-image and its twin, low self-esteem. Many celebrities, most notably Princess Diana, prior to her tragic death in Paris, have suffered from anorexia and bulimia while under the relentless pursuit and scrutiny of the paparazzi. All of the emphasis is on the physical development while the spiritual aspect of our development is virtually neglected. Your body, mind, and spirit must be nurtured and cared for equally if you want to uncover the true happiness which you deserve and for which you were created.

Coach Pitino said his team needed to put themselves in the "best possible position to succeed." The same is true for all of us. We need to trust God while we have the opportunity. We need to put ourselves in the "best possible position to succeed" by resolving to trust our Savior and making it part of our daily routine to spend a few minutes reading a passage from the "Owner's Manual." We all need to "strike while the iron is hot" and **trust the Spirit of Jesus** to provide for all our needs—physical, emotional, and spiritual. Then, we will truly be in the best position to succeed in becoming the complete, mature women and men that God wants us to become.

Remember, keep your ADF tuned to the **Spirit** within you!

> Only you have the power within you.
> Just believe in yourself and see the path
> > before you
> Stop the rain and turn the tide
> If only you use the power within you
> You can draw on what you have within you
> Somewhere deep inside. . .

Only You from *Starlight Express*
Lyrics by Richard Stilgoe
Music by Andrew Lloyd Webber
copyright 1984 The Really Useful Group Ltd., London.
All Rights Reserved. International Copyright Secured.
Reproduced by permission of the copyright owner.

David Huddleston

Spiritual Jetstreams

Chapter 6

Total Reliance Upon The Spirit

In the same way, the Spirit helps us in our weakness. We do not know what we ought to pray for, but the Spirit himself intercedes for us with groans that words cannot express. And he who searches our hearts knows the mind of the Spirit, because the Spirit intercedes for the saints in accordance with God's will.

And we know that in all things God works for the good of those who love him, who have been called according to his purpose. For those God foreknew he also predestined to be conformed to the likeness of his Son, that he might be the firstborn among many brothers. And those he predestined he also called; those he called, he also justified; those he justified, he also glorified.

What, then, shall we say in response to this? If God is for us, who can be against us? He who did not spare his own Son, but gave him up for us all-how will he not also, along with him, graciously give us all things? Who will bring any charge against those whom God has chosen? It is God who justifies. Who is he that condemns? Christ Jesus, who died--more than that, who was raised to life--is at the right hand of God and is also interceding for us. Who shall separate us from the love of Christ? Shall trouble or hardship or persecution or famine or nakedness or danger or sword? As it is written:

"For your sake we face death all day long;

we are considered as sheep to be slaughtered."

No, in all these things we are more than conquerors through him who loved us. For I am convinced that neither death nor life, neither angels nor demons, neither the present nor the future, nor any powers, neither height nor depth, nor anything else in all creation, will be able to separate us from the love of God that is in Christ Jesus our Lord.
(Romans 8:26-39)

"And we know that in all things God works for the good of those who love him, who have been called according to his purpose."
(Romans 8:28)

"A cat, a dog, and a duck. That's all you need to fly IFR. Just forget all those fancy instruments." said my crusty old flight instructor, Wally Hampton, as we prepared for my first IFR (instrument flight rules) lesson. I would be wearing a "hood" soon after takeoff in order to learn to fly the airplane without visual references to the outside. Instead, I would be forced to rely on the flight instruments and trust them in order to keep the aircraft under control. The basic instruments in our Cessna 150 were the artificial horizon, turn and bank indicator, altimeter, airspeed indicator, vertical speed indicator, and omni (omnidirectional aid to navigation). The first lesson was particularly difficult because I had to totally disregard what my senses were telling me about the attitude of the airplane (whether we were climbing, descending, turning, or straight and level). Your mind will play tricks on you when you're under the hood (or in the clouds!) and it is critical to learn to trust your instruments.

My instructor's joke about "a cat, a dog, and a duck" was meant to ease my anxiety about learning to fly IFR. The theory is that all you need inside the cockpit to fly through the clouds are:

> A cat - to keep you right-side-up. (A cat will always come down right-side-up even if you toss it into the air blindfolded.)

A dog - to keep the cat awake.

and

A duck - to help you land.

When coming in for a landing and the visibility is so poor that you can't see the runway, all you have to do is just watch the duck. When it spreads its wings and flares (raises its nose) for landing, you flare!

I guess he was telling me to trust them for a safe flight.

The question that concerns us today is, "Who are you gonna trust?" Who are you going to ultimately put your faith and trust in to guide you safely through all the choices you must make in your life? Are you going to rely on your own wisdom and knowledge or will you decide to **allow God through the Holy Spirit** to give you a safe trip?

The thoroughbred jockey, Pat Day, was being interviewed in the winner's circle after winning the Preakness Stakes at Pimlico in Maryland (the second jewel in racing's Triple Crown). Pat had been taken off of the horse which he had wanted to ride (the horse he had ridden in the Kentucky Derby just 3 weeks before) and had been replaced in favor of another jockey by the trainer. The trainer thought his horse would have a better chance of winning the Preakness if Day was replaced. Pat was bitterly disappointed, but was given another mount. It turned out to be providential for him however, since he subsequently won the race to everyone's surprise. When the announcer asked Pat how he felt about being replaced on his original horse, Pat answered, "The Bible is the inspired Word of God and Romans 8:28 says: 'We know that in all things God works for the good of those who love him, who have been called according to his purpose.' I believe that God allowed this to happen for a reason and I am trusting him for everything that happens to me."

    The announcer was indignant that this hall-of-fame jockey was talking about his faith in God on national television. He quickly cut him off by making a reference to Pat's life before he became a Christian and then abruptly ended the interview without allowing Pat to say anything else. However, Pat Day had made his point for the whole world to hear. Instead of criticizing the trainer who had removed him from his Derby horse, Pat was praising the Lord for being there to take care of him and for using these circumstances for his own good. He refused to feel like a victim. He put his trust in the Holy Spirit and not in the owner or trainer. He believed that God would work this out for his ultimate benefit so he refused to worry about it and he didn't blame others for what had happened to him. (Pat always raises his whip above his head, looks up to heaven, and thanks the Lord in the winner's circle after every race he wins!)

Andrew Lloyd Webber and Tim Rice in their 1968 musical, *Joseph And The Amazing Technicolor® Dreamcoat*, retell the book of Genesis account of Jacob's eleventh son, Joseph. Joseph was Jacob's favorite son since he was born to Rachel in Jacob's old age. He made the mistake of showing favoritism to Joseph by giving him "a coat of many colors." Joseph's ten older brothers hated him and were jealous as a result. Joseph had two dreams in which his brothers were depicted as bowing down to him as their ruler. This made them hate him all the more and they later sold him into slavery to some merchants who were traveling to Egypt. The brothers then took the "coat of many colors" and dipped it into the blood of a goat they had killed before taking it back to their father under the deception that Joseph had been killed.

When Joseph arrived in Egypt, he was sold to Potiphar who was Pharaoh's captain of the guard. Potiphar saw that the Lord was with Joseph and gave him success in everything he did, so he put him in charge of his household. Soon after, Potiphar's wife tempted Joseph and tried to seduce him. When he refused, she made up a story about him saying that he had tried to seduce her. As a result, Joseph was thrown into prison for several years. He eventually was freed after he interpreted Pharaoh's dreams concerning the seven years of famine that were to come. Pharaoh was so appreciative that he put Joseph in charge of the whole land of Egypt as his second-in-command. Joseph had successfully stored up grain prior to the famine so that the people would be fed.

After the famine had begun and had spread over all of Egypt as well as Canaan where Joseph's family lived, Jacob sent his ten older sons to Egypt to buy grain and bring it home. He kept his twelfth son, Benjamin, at home so that no harm would come to him since he was so much younger. When the ten brothers arrived in Egypt they went to the governor of the land who could sell them grain. The governor was Joseph. Joseph recognized his brothers, but they did not realize it was him. He then tested them by telling them to go back home and get their youngest brother and bring him to Egypt to verify that they were not spies sent from Canaan. They did as he said and when they returned with Benjamin they were given a royal welcome and a feast in their honor.

When Joseph could no longer control himself, he made himself known to his brothers and said:

I am your brother, Joseph, the one you sold into Egypt! And now, do not be distressed and do not be angry with yourselves for selling me here, because it was to save lives that God sent me ahead of you...to preserve for you a remnant on earth and to save your lives by a great deliverance. (Genesis 45:4-7)

He did not return evil for evil. He did not hate his brothers and seek revenge. Instead, he gave God the glory by saying that it was for God's own purposes and Joseph's own good that he had been betrayed by his brothers and sold into slavery. Joseph then forgave all his brothers for what they had done to him and he put his arms around them and kissed them all. They were then sent back to Canaan to get Jacob and all their families so they could return to Egypt where Joseph would give them all the food and land they needed to live on for the rest of their lives.

Jacob and all his family subsequently came to Egypt and remained there where he died after 17 years. (This was the migration of the nation of Israel to Egypt where they would remain in captivity for 400 years until Moses led them back to Canaan. The twelve tribes of Israel and the nation itself spring from Jacob's twelve sons. Jesus was descended from Judah, who was one of these sons). When Joseph's brothers discovered that their father had died, they were afraid that Joseph would hold a grudge and they threw themselves before him and pleaded for mercy. But Joseph spoke kindly to them and said:

Don't be afraid. Am I in the place of God? You intended to harm me, but God intended it for good to accomplish what is now being done, the saving of many lives. So then don't be afraid. I will provide for you and your children. (Genesis 50:19-21)

He did not punish them. He did not hold a grudge. He was not bitter! Instead, he attributed all that had happened in his life to God's divine providence. All his dreams had come true! As a result, the nation of Israel was preserved, Judah lived and became an ancestor of Jesus, and you and I are saved today! Just before Joseph died at 110 years of age he made his brothers promise to take his body back to the promised land. 400 years later, his dream came true when Moses took his bones with him during the exodus from Egypt back to Israel.

Lloyd Webber and Rice close their show with Joseph singing *Any Dream Will Do*.

>I closed my eyes drew back the curtain
>To see for certain what I thought I knew
>Far far away someone was weeping
>But the world was sleeping
>Any dream will do
>
>I wore my coat
>With golden lining
>Bright colours shining
>Wonderful and new
>And in the east
>The dawn was breaking
>The world was waking
>Any dream will do
>
>A crash of drums a flash of light
>My golden coat flew out of sight
>The colours faded into darkness
>I was left alone
>
>May I return to the beginning
>The light is dimming
>And the dream is, too
>
>The world and I
>We are still waiting
>Still hesitating
>Any dream will do*

In the end, after a lifetime of trouble and disappointments (and trusting God) Joseph's dream of being reunited with his family and returning to his homeland finally came true. God really does work all things for the good of those who love him and are called according to his purpose!

As a young student pilot, I had to rely on my flight instruments and trust them to keep the plane on course. As a jockey, Pat Day has learned to trust God to take care of him in all circumstances. As a young man sold into slavery by his brothers, Joseph put his faith in the Lord to work out all the problems he faced. Who will you trust to help you through all of life's circumstances? **Who are you gonna trust?** to give you a smooth, safe trip and bring you in for a nice soft landing at your final destination?

"...God's Spirit within us is actually praying for us in those agonizing longings which never find words. And God who knows the heart's secrets understands, of course, the Spirit's intention as he prays for those who love God. Moreover we know that to those who love God, who are called according to his plan, everything that happens fits into a pattern for good." (Romans 8:26-28 Phillips)

*"Any Dream Will Do" from "Joseph And The Amazing Technicolor® Dreamcoat"
Lyrics by Tim Rice. Music by Andrew Lloyd Webber.
Copyright 1968 The Really Useful Music Group Ltd., London
All Rights Reserved. International Copyright Secured.
Reproduced By Permission Of The Copyright Owner.

Spiritual Jetstreams

Chapter 7

Achieving Spiritual Maturity

Consider it pure joy, my brothers, whenever you face trials of many kinds, because you know that the testing of your faith develops perseverance. Perseverance must finish its work so that you may be mature and complete, not lacking anything. If any of you lacks wisdom, he should ask God, who gives generously to all without finding fault, and it will be given to him. But when he asks, he must believe and not doubt, because he who doubts is like a wave of the sea, blown and tossed by the wind. That man should not think he will receive anything from the Lord; he is a double-minded man, unstable in all he does.

The brother in humble circumstances ought to take pride in his high position. But the one who is rich should take pride in his low position, because he will pass away like a wild flower. For the sun rises with scorching heat and withers the plant; its blossom falls and its beauty is destroyed. In the same way, the rich man will fade away even while he goes about his business.
(James 1:2-11)

Happy is the person who remains faithful under trials, because when he succeeds in passing such a test, he will receive as his reward the life which God has promised to those who love him.
(James 1:12 TEV)

The ceiling was 400 feet and visibility one mile with fog and drizzle as we circled overhead at 10,000 feet waiting for our turn to begin our descent and approach to runway 18 at New York's La Guardia Airport. We had been in a holding pattern for nearly an hour when approach control finally cleared us to begin our descent down to 5000 feet. We would be approaching over Long Island Sound at night with a rain-slickened runway awaiting our touchdown. Our flight had departed Montreal at 9:00 PM on what we thought would be a routine trip to New York. The plane was full of business people and vacationers anxious to get to New York to begin the weekend. But, we had already been delayed for two hours due to deteriorating weather conditions which had forced us to hold over upper New York State and return to Montreal because of dwindling fuel on board. After refueling, we had taken off again only to be caught in a holding pattern once again along with several other big jets above and below us.

If you've ever experienced a delay in landing at your destination while flying, then you know what it feels like to be "caught in a holding pattern." That's the condition air traffic controllers put you in when the weather is a problem or there's too much air traffic at your destination airport. As a Boeing 727 pilot, I've been forced to hold for as much as an hour, stacked up over the New York area while waiting to land at La Guardia. It's a very frustrating and helpless feeling as you circle overhead while sandwiched between aircraft 2000 feet above and below. You're wasting precious fuel and you're not getting your passengers to their destination at the appointed time to meet friends and family or make critical connections to continue their trips. You make endless 20 mile long holding patterns while waiting for the weather to clear or planes below you to complete their approach and landing.

It seems like such a waste of time and money to say nothing of trying everyone's patience. There are going to be many times in your life when you are going to feel like you, too, are "caught in a holding pattern." You will most likely feel very frustrated and helpless during those times when life throws you a curve and you're forced to just sit and wait for your turn to get on with your life. The most important thing to remember is that the way you respond during these times is what will ultimately determine what kind of person you become. If you can use these experiences to develop **patience** and **perseverance**, then you will have gone a long way toward learning to grow into **spiritual maturity** which is what we all need to be working toward.

I read not long ago of an 88 year old woman from Mississippi (now deceased) who was afraid to fly. Fear of flying is a very common phobia primarily because it can make you feel that you are not in control of the situation. This "loss of control" feeling can produce anxiety which can result in a panic attack for many people. As a jet pilot, I have become so accustomed to getting in the cockpit and taking off that it is just as natural for me as getting in my car and turning on the ignition to go somewhere. But, I also realize that not all my passengers feel that way. They don't all fly every day and for many of them each flight is a new obstacle to be overcome.

The 88 year old woman I mentioned had never

been on an airplane in her entire life. As a matter of fact, she had only been outside of her home state of Mississippi once in her life. The thought of getting on an airplane was just too much for her. She had lived a very quiet and happy life taking in other people's laundry and washing it in her house in Hattiesburg. However, she was forced to overcome her fear of flying because she was in such great demand all over the country and her preferred mode of transportation, the train, was just too slow. When she did have to fly, she liked to sit by a window so she could look down on the clouds. In one of the greatest displays of charity I have ever heard of, this woman gave her life savings of $150,000 to the University of Southern Mississippi so that black students with financial hardships would be able to go to college. She used the money accumulated over a lifetime of hard work to finance scholarships for needy students even though she was suffering from arthritis and living on Social Security. She was living in the same house where she has been all her life and where she had lived alone for the past thirty years since her aunt, who lived with her, died. Because of her generosity, she was in demand by organizations all over the country who wanted to honor her. Her name was Oseola McCarty. She was a Godly woman. She had learned to persevere. She read her tattered old Bible every day and the Holy Spirit was her constant companion. Miss McCarty had remained faithful to the Lord throughout all the trials and hardships in her life and her unbelievable generosity and compassion for young people just starting out in life was evidence of her close walk with God. She had grown into **spiritual maturity**. She had learned to **trust God** to satisfy all her needs.

Jesus' brother, James, who had become a leader in the early church in Jerusalem, wrote a letter to his fellow believers encouraging them to look on it as "pure joy" whenever they experienced difficult situations. James pointed out that **testing** of our faith develops **perseverance** which then leads to **spiritual maturity**. In other words, it is our attitude toward our circumstances that determines the effect that life's events subsequently have on us. If we complain and grieve over everything that happens to us, in the end we will become bitter and angry and filled with resentment as we develop the expectation of defeat and unhappiness. However, if we look at difficult circumstances as opportunities for growth and remember that the Lord allows certain things to happen to us for our own benefit, the end result will be a higher level of spiritual maturity as we seek to do God's will by **allowing the Holy Spirit to guide and direct** us through all the storms of life. If we follow our natural instincts and try to solve all our problems by our own means, we will fail miserably. All of our knowledge, cleverness, or intelligence will not be sufficient when we are besieged by those difficult times which inevitably come to each person. Secular counseling will not suffice. Prescription drugs will not suffice, though they may help in certain situations, particularly depression. Needless to say, the use of illegal drugs will not suffice.

Just as our 727 successfully touched down at La Guardia that "dark and stormy night" after being caught in a holding pattern for so long, we can all arrive safely at God's special destination which he has planned for us if we will allow His Holy Spirit to guide and direct us through each day we live, no matter what happens.

    He wants to be our guide, our helper, and our constant companion every day. It is up to us to invite Him in!

Spiritual Jetstreams

Chapter 8

Discovering Your Spiritual Gifts

Now about spiritual gifts, brothers, I do not want you to be ignorant. You know that when you were pagans, somehow or other you were influenced and led astray to mute idols. Therefore I tell you that no one who is speaking by the Spirit of God says, "Jesus be cursed," and no one can say, "Jesus is Lord," except by the Holy Spirit.

There are different kinds of gifts but the same Spirit. There are different kinds of service, but the same Lord. There are different kinds of working, but the same God works all of them in all men.

Now to each one the manifestation of the Spirit is given for the common good. To one there is given through the Spirit the message of wisdom, to another the message of knowledge by means of the same Spirit, to another faith by the same Spirit, to another gifts of healing by that one Spirit, to another miraculous powers, to another prophecy, to another distinguishing between spirits, to another speaking in different kinds of tongues, and to still another the interpretation of tongues. All these are the work of one and the same Spirit, and he gives them to each one, just as he determines.

The body is a unit, though it is made up of many parts; and though all its parts are many, they form one body. So it is with Christ. For we were all baptized by one Spirit into one body-whether Jews or Greeks, slave or free -and we were all given the one Spirit to drink.

Now the body is not made up of one part but of many. If the foot should say, "Because I am not a hand, I do not belong to the body," it would not for that reason cease to be part of the body. And if the ear should say, "Because I am not an eye, I do not belong to the body," it would not for that reason cease to be part of the body. If the whole body were an eye, where would the sense of hearing be? But in fact God has arranged the parts in the body, every one of them, just as he wanted them to be. If they were all one part, where would the body be? As it is, there are many parts, but one body.

The eye cannot say to the hand, "I don't need you!" On the contrary, those parts of the body that seem to be weaker are indispensable, and the parts that we think are less honorable we treat with special honor. And the parts that are unpresentable are treated with special modesty, while our presentable parts need no special treatment. But God has combined the members of the body and has given greater honor to the parts that lacked it, so that there should be no division in the body, but that its parts should have equal concern for each other. If one part suffers, every part suffers with it; if one part is honored, every part rejoices with it.

Now you are the body of Christ, and each one of you is a part of it. And in the church God has

appointed first of all apostles, second prophets, third teachers, then workers of miracles, also those having gifts of healing, those able to help others, those with gifts of administration, and those speaking in different kinds of tongues. Are all apostles? Are all prophets? Are all teachers? Do all work miracles? Do all have gifts of healing? Do all speak in tongues? Do all interpret? But eagerly desire the greater gifts.
(1 Cor 12:1-31)

Now God gives us many kinds of special abilities, but it is the same Holy Spirit who is the source of them all. There are different kinds of service to God, but it is the same Lord we are serving. There are many ways in which God works in our lives, but it is the same God who does the work in and through all of us who are his. The Holy Spirit displays God's power through each of us as a means of helping the entire church.
(1 Cor 12:4-7 TLB)

In a thick Spanish accent, the air traffic controller in Caracas said to me, "Quatro quatro uno, cleared to land at the Maiquetia Airport." Maiquetia is a resort town located on the northern shore of South America. The airport for Caracas, Venezuela, is in Maiquetia and has an east-west runway at the foot of a 6000' high mountain chain (Cordillera de la Costa) overlooking the Caribbean. The prevailing winds are from the east so we always landed toward the east into the wind, always at night, and frequently in fog and rain depending on the time of year.

The check Captain said, "Let's run the checklist," as I turned our 727 onto a five-mile final approach for landing. This would be my first landing outside of the training simulators and practice field where we did our "bounces" as they are called prior to earning our wings. The "bounces" were actually 3 touch-and-go landings we were required to execute to the satisfaction of our flight instructor before we were released to fly "the line" as pilots on regularly scheduled routes. "The line" is the system the airlines use which allows flight crews to bid on specific sequences, or lines, for the upcoming month. As I looked at the runway lights in the distance through fog and drizzle it seemed impossible to me that we would ever be able to stop the airplane after landing on so short a runway. It was 9000' long and more than adequate for our aircraft, but appeared like a tiny postage stamp when viewed at night from 3000' altitude and five miles out. We were approaching at 150 knots and my heart rate felt like it was equal to our airspeed! My hands were sweating profusely and I kept drying them on my pants in order to try and hold onto the yoke and throttles. This was not exactly the calmest moment of my life since I needed the approval of the check Captain when we got back to our home base in Miami if I was to be fully qualified to fly.

As the Second Officer called out the "Before Landing-Final" checklist we responded as the approach continued:

No Smoke	"On"
Gear Down	"3 Green, Pressure and Quantity (hydraulic fluid) Checked"
Anti-Skid	"Checked"
Auto Brakes	"On"
Auto Speed Brakes	"Armed Green Light"
Fuel Panel	"Set"
Wing Flaps	"30 Degrees and Leading Edge Devices Green Light"
	"Checklist complete."

Now it was time for the fun to begin. I have always felt a little uneasy when communicating with air traffic controllers in Latin America. While they are for the most part very professional and conscientious, their broken English mixed in with Spanish was a cause for concern. This, along with the fact that we frequently were unable to get them to respond for long periods of time gave rise to their perceived philosophy of "You all be careful out there now, you hear!" which basically means that you are on your own so watch out for other planes! So when I heard "Quatro quatro uno

(441), cleared to land at Maiquetia," I immediately went on high alert for other traffic in the area. This only added to my anxiety of making my first real live landing with passengers aboard. After departing the Miami International Airport our route had brought us over Bimini Island and then Andros Island in the Bahamas before heading down over Port-au-Prince, Haiti and the Caribbean Sea. Further south we passed near the "ABC Islands" of Aruba, Bonaire, and Curacao on our descent into Caracas. In the distance, Maracaibo sparkled like a twinkling distant star where the South American continent meets the Caribbean blue. En route I had studied the approach plate for Maiquetia until I knew it like the back of my hand and I had mentally gone over all the checklists (Descent-In-Range, Before Landing-Final, etc.) in hopes of not making too big a blunder.

Whenever I meet someone for the first time I find myself subconsciously taking their "spiritual temperature." I run my own checklist wondering if perhaps this person has the gift of wisdom or knowledge or discernment or some other special ability given by the Holy Spirit. Why has God chosen to let our paths cross at this particular point in time? Is he going to use us to accomplish his purpose in some unique way or is this just a chance meeting of no particular consequence?

The apostle Paul discusses the **Charismata** or **gifts of the Spirit** in Romans 12, 1 Cor 12, and Ephesians 4. These differ from the **fruits of the Spirit** (love, joy, peace, patience, kindness, goodness, faithfulness, gentleness, and self-control) found in Galatians 5 in that God has given every believer the ability to do certain things well. While the fruits of the Spirit are the Christ-like characteristics which every believer should have as he or she surrenders to the Holy Spirit and allows him to produce his fruit in his or her life, the gifts of the Spirit are given individually to each believer. While we cannot possess **all** the Spiritual gifts, it is critical for us to discover which gifts we have been blessed with so that we can put them to work for the Savior.

Each of us has been given different gifts because we each have different work to do in order to join with all God's children in making the Lord's work complete in our world.

In Romans 12:6-8, Paul lists the following Spiritual gifts:

<u>Prophesying</u> - the ability to preach
<u>Serving</u> - the ability to minister to people
<u>Teaching</u> - the gift of illuminating God's Word
<u>Encouraging</u> - the ability to inspire and reassure
<u>Giving</u> - contributing to the needs of others
<u>Leadership</u> - providing guidance and direction
<u>Compassion</u> - showing mercy and giving comfort to those who are hurting

In 1 Corinthians 12:4-11, Paul lists:

<u>Wisdom</u> - the ability to communicate spiritual wisdom or give wise advice
<u>Knowledge</u> (or Word of Knowledge) - the ability to communicate practical truth not derived from sensory input

<u>Faith</u> - extraordinary reliance on God
<u>Healing</u> - the ability to perform healing miracles unexplained by medical science
<u>Miracles</u> - the ability to perform supernatural phenomena
<u>Preaching</u> - the gift of publicly proclaiming the Gospel of Christ
<u>Discernment</u> - the ability to distinguish between evil spirits and the Holy Spirit
<u>Tongues</u> - the ability to speak in languages never learned
<u>Interpretation of Tongues</u> - the ability to understand a language never learned

In 1 Corinthians 12:28, we find:

<u>Apostleship</u> - the gift given to those set apart by God and sent out on a mission to evangelize the world
<u>Prophecy</u> - the ability to proclaim new revelation from God or forecast a future event
<u>Teaching</u> - the gift of illuminating God's Word
<u>Miracles</u> - the ability to perform supernatural phenomena
<u>Healing</u> - the ability to perform healing miracles unexplained by medical science
<u>Helps</u> - the ability to help others
<u>Administration</u> - the ability to get others to work together
<u>Tongues</u> - the ability to speak in languages never learned

In Ephesians 4:11, Paul completes the Charismata:

Apostleship - the gift given to those set apart by God and sent out on a mission to evangelize the world
Prophecy - the ability to proclaim new revelation from God or forecast a future event
Evangelism - the ability to win people to Christ
Discipleship - the ability to pastor and teach God's people

The point is that the **gifts** of the Spirit (you have at least one and probably several!) and the **fruits** of the Spirit should work together in your life as you seek the Lord's calling upon you and his purpose for your life. That's why it's so important to help God's people discover their Spiritual gifts and understand how God uses them. If you look carefully at the life of Jesus you will quickly discover that he manifested all of the gifts of the Spirit in his life (except for tongues and the interpretation of tongues). Some believe that these two gifts were necessary before the word of God was written and that they no longer exist today. Other theologians and certain denominations seek to discredit all the gifts and teach that no one possesses any of the "Charismata" today and that they all disappeared with the Apostolic Age nearly 2000 years ago. I can find no Biblical foundation for either argument and I really think that it tends to put God into a box and limit what he can do through the life of a true believer. I have seen from my own experience that when Spirit-filled Christians come together and seek to serve the Lord with a sincere and humble heart, that's when miracles happen! God is in the miracle business and if he chooses to give a particular spiritual gift to someone for his own purposes, that's his business. I would never presume to take away from God's Word what is so clearly there for our benefit and his eternal purposes.

Following are some brief guidelines to help you in discovering your Spiritual gifts:

1. Realize that God wants to fill you with his Holy Spirit. Luke 11:9,13: *Jesus said, "Ask and it will be given to you; seek and you will find; knock and the door will be opened to you...If you then, though you are evil, know how to give good gifts to your children, how much more will your Father in heaven give the Holy Spirit to those who ask him!"*

2. Discipline yourself to get alone with God every day for a few minutes and ask him to fill you with his Holy Spirit. Gal 5:16: *"Obey only the Holy Spirit's instructions."* (TLB)

3. Ask the Lord to show you what your Spiritual gifts are and then begin putting them into practice. If you are really gifted in a particular area, spirit-filled Christians will soon affirm your gifts as your work begins to bear fruit. 1 Cor 14:1: *"Follow the way of love and eagerly desire spiritual gifts..."* NIV, *"Let love be your greatest aim; nevertheless, ask also for the special abilities the Holy Spirit gives..."* (TLB) Try to find a Spiritual mentor to encourage you and to help you discover your gifts!

4. Believe that you have equal access to the Spiritual gifts that everyone does. As a believer, made in God's own image, the gifts of the Spirit are equally attainable by you. None are reserved for a select few. There are no limitations based on gender, race, age, denomination, etc.

As you begin to discover your spiritual gifts and put them into use, remember that we do not all have the same gifts and we should never feel that our personal gifts are any more or less important than someone else's. Paul cautioned in I Cor 12, that we should remember that just as our bodies have many parts and the parts make up one body when they are put together, it is the same with the "body" of Christ. The Holy Spirit has fitted us all together into one body and we all have different gifts, but they are all given by the same Holy Spirit!

Just as I had to learn to "run the checklist" before I successfully landed that 727 for the first time (WHEW!), you need to run your own "spiritual checklist" to determine the special abilities which the Holy Spirit has given to you and those around you. The gifts you discover will literally change your life forever and the world will be a better place because you're in it and God is working through you to accomplish his eternal purposes.

David Huddleston

Chapter 9

Marriage And The Spirit

When Jesus finished saying these things, he left Galilee and went to the territory of Judea on the other side of the Jordan River. Large crowds followed him, and he healed them there.

Some Pharisees came to him and tried to trap him by asking, "Does our Law allow a man to divorce his wife for whatever reason he wishes?"

Jesus answered, "Haven't you read the scripture that says that in the beginning the Creator made people male and female? And God said, 'For this reason a man will leave his father and mother and unite with his wife, and the two will become one.' So they are no longer two, but one. Man must not separate, then, what God has joined together."

The Pharisees asked him, "Why, then, did Moses give the law for a man to hand his wife a divorce notice and send her away?"

Jesus answered, "Moses gave you permission to divorce your wives because you are so hard to teach. But it was not like that at the time of creation. I tell you, then, that any man who divorces his wife for any cause other than her unfaithfulness, commits adultery if he marries some other woman."

His disciples said to him, "If this is how it is between a man and his wife, it is better not to marry."

Jesus answered, "This teaching does not apply to everyone, but only to those to whom God has given it. For there are different reasons why men cannot marry: some, because they were born that way; others, because men made them that way; and others do not marry for the sake of the Kingdom of heaven. Let him who can accept this teaching do so."
(Mt 19:1-12 TEV)

"Submit to one another out of reverence for Christ."
(Eph 5:21)

It was a huge idea. Huge! I would buy my wife a Dustbuster for her birthday. She would love it! Even cherish it. It would allow her to save time cleaning the house and dusting those hard to get to places. It would be great. She would love me for it.

This brilliant epiphany came to me while en route returning from a layover in Panama. We had been gone for three days and had stayed in the bullet-riddled hotel which had been under attack only one week prior by U.S. armed forces. The invasion of Panama for purposes of deposing military dictator Manuel Noriega had left visible scars on the face of Panama City. We could still see where the assault forces had come ashore on the Pacific side of the canal. Large caliber machine gun bullet holes were visible all along our route down to the hotel and into the lobby of the hotel itself. After a short stay there, we had headed back to Miami and, while enroute, cruising over the Caribbean at 38,000 feet, I was trying to think of just the right gift to give to my wife for her birthday. I had seen those commercials on television for the labor-saving Dustbuster and I just knew this would be the perfect gift for my wife. It was brilliant, inspired. She never touched it!

The problem was, of course, that I gave my wife a gift that I thought she should have without considering her wants or needs. In Ephesians, chapter 5, the apostle Paul gives some timeless advice for husbands and wives, "Don't act thoughtlessly, but try to find out and do whatever the Lord wants you to. Don't drink too much wine for many evils lie along that path; be filled instead with the Holy Spirit and controlled by him. Honor Christ by submitting to each other." Ephesians

5:17-18, 21(TLB) The NIV translates verse 21, **"Submit to one another out of reverence for Christ."** The idea here is mutual subjection between wife and husband. I really believe that this is the key to a happy marriage. It is the idea of **co-regency** for women and men within the bond of marriage. I really think that every couple needs to make the Holy Spirit the active third partner in their marriage if they have any hope for a successful and happy marriage. Without the Spirit's help, the conflicts and problems which inevitably come along later in the marriage will be much more difficult, if not impossible, to resolve.

If you are unmarried, but you would like to be married, let me suggest that you ask the Holy Spirit to help you to find your husband or wife. 1 John 5:14 reads that "if you ask anything according to his (God's) will he hears us." The evangelist, Billy Graham, put it very succinctly when he said, "If you take an unbeliever for a mate, you also get the devil for your father-in-law." Far too much grief has been caused by Christians marrying unbelievers. Make sure that whomever you choose to marry is a believer. The Bible tells us in 1 Corinthians 7:39, "The wife is part of her husband as long as he lives. If her husband dies, she may marry again, but only if she marries a Christian." Marriage is hard enough without bringing in the extra conflict of faith (or lack of faith) into the equation. Part of the problem here is that many more women have a deep personal relationship with Christ than do men. In a recent poll it was found that women are more likely than men to be thankful for their faith by a margin of roughly forty percent to 30 percent. This reinforces the idea that women are taught from an early age to nurture relationships much more than men are. Therefore, as they mature it is much more natural and easier for women to develop close personal relationships with others. And, ultimately, women more readily can develop a deep personal relationship with the Holy Spirit than can men.

In Matthew 19:4-6, Jesus said, "Haven't you read the scripture that says that 'In the beginning the Creator made people male and female?' And God said, 'For this reason a man will leave his father and mother and unite with his wife and the two will become one.' So they are no longer two but one. Man must not separate what God has joined together." God has ordained that the marriage of women and men will be a holy union blessed by him and meant to last a lifetime. We must look at marriage as more of a marathon than a sprint and seek the help of the Holy Spirit every day of our lives together. It is critical to make the care and nurture of your marriage your top priority. Inevitably, as the marriage begins to mature, it comes under increasing stress. As both the wife and the husband begin working outside the home, caring for the children along with all of the financial stresses that come into play almost always produce conflicts which, if not dealt with properly and constructively, can undermine the very foundation of the relationship between the wife and husband.

A few years ago in the Florida Everglades, Eastern Airlines flight 421, a Lockheed L-1011 Tristar was approaching to land at the Miami International Airport. As the First Officer attempted to lower the landing gear, he noticed that he got two green lights for each of the main landing gears but the green light that would indicate that the nose wheel was down and locked in place did not come on. It ultimately turned out that it was merely a blown light bulb in the green indicator light that was the problem and that the nose gear was down and locked in place. However, this tiny ten-cent light bulb began a tragic chain of events which led to the deaths of scores of people on a clear cloudless night in the Everglades just west of Miami. Because they did not get the three green indicator lights as required for landing, the pilots were forced to divert into a holding pattern just a few miles west of Miami International Airport. As they entered the holding pattern the autopilot was engaged and programmed to keep the aircraft at a constant safe altitude above the ground while the crew attempted to determine if in fact all three landing gears were safely down and locked in place. This illustrates how a seemingly inconsequential problem can turn into a disaster if not properly handled. While in the holding pattern, the captain attempted to check the light bulb on the nosegear indicator light, and after removing it and trying to reinsert the bulb, he succeeded in jamming the bulb in the socket so that it could not become illuminated. While another crew member lowered himself into the area just below the flight deck to make a visual inspection of the nosegear, one of the pilots accidentally bumped against the aircraft yoke inadvertently disengaging the autopilot. As the giant wide-body Tristar began a slow, circling descent over the pitch black Everglades, no one seemed to notice that the altimeter indicated that they were descending. As the crew continued to wrestle with the problem of the landing gear indicator light, alarm bells and flashing lights went off indicating that the autopilot was disengaged and that the aircraft was dangerously close to the ground. One of the pilots finally looked up at his instruments and noticed that something didn't look right. He attempted to pull up but it was too late. The wingtip of the aircraft hit the marshy surface of the Everglades as the spiral continued and the L-1011 subsequently crashed into waist-deep, alligator-infested water and broke apart in a catastrophic crash.

Sometimes in a marriage things can become so routine that it seems like you are just going along on autopilot and that no one is really "minding the store." When this happens, sometimes even the smallest, most insignificant problems become blown way out of proportion and it's as if the eruption of Mount St. Helens has been revisited.

Following are some suggestions to help when this situation occurs:

1. First of all, be careful what you say. Remember that what is said can never be unsaid. Matthew 12:36 says that, "You will have to give account on the day of judgment for every careless word you have spoken."

2. Don't let your tongue control you. James 1:26 says, "If anyone considers himself religious and yet does not keep a tight rein on his tongue, he deceives himself and his religion is worthless."

3. James 1:19 says, "Everyone should be quick to listen, slow to speak, and slow to become

angry. Man's anger does not bring about the righteous life that God desires." If the wife and husband could both learn to practice this, it would go a long way toward preventing minor disagreements from escalating into World War III.

4. Don't hold a grudge. Colossians 3:13 states, "Bear with each other and forgive whatever grievances you may have against one another. Forgive as the Lord forgave you." As a wife or husband you have a perfect right to become angry at times. It is not a sin to become angry. We know from the New Testament that Jesus became angry at times, particularly with the moneylenders in the temple. He got mad, threw them all out and turned their tables upside down. But we must be very careful not to let our anger lead us into sin. A crucial principle here is that a person should listen to his or her feelings but never be controlled by them. We are told in Proverbs 16:32, "He who is slow to anger is greater than the mighty. He who rules his spirit is better than he who captures a city." Proverbs 19:11, "A man's discretion makes him slow to anger." In other words we need to be sensitive to our feelings but never controlled by them.

We tend to mechanically repeat the part of the Lord's prayer that says, "Forgive us our sins as we forgive those who have sinned against us," but very few of us stop to consider the consequences of what we are saying. The Amplified Bible's interpretation of the verse immediately following the Lord's prayer (Mt 6:15) says, "If we do not give up our resentment or grudges, God will not forgive our sins." You see, clinging stubbornly to resentment is very destructive to us because it blocks God's forgiveness. This scriptural principle helps explain the relationship between guilt and unresolved anger. **I am convinced that most of the emotional problems in Christians are caused by two things: First, failure to receive forgiveness and, secondly, failure to give forgiveness.** In Mt 18:21-35, Jesus tells the parable of the unmerciful servant and gives the consequences of an unforgiving heart. There was a man who owed his master more than a million dollars, but when he begged for the debt to be cancelled so that he and his family could be set free, his master took pity on him, cancelled the debt, and let them go. But, when the freed servant went out, he found one of his former fellow servants who owed him roughly ten dollars and he began to choke him and demand that he pay him back the debt. His fellow servant fell to his knees and asked for mercy. However, the man refused and instead had his fellow servant thrown into prison. When the master found out about this he called the freed servant in and said, "'You wicked servant! I cancelled that debt of yours because you begged me to. Shouldn't you have had mercy on your fellow servant just as I had on you?' In anger, his master turned the man over to his jailers to be tortured until he should pay back all he owed. This is how our Heavenly Father will treat each of you unless you forgive your brother from your heart."

    You see, when we fail to accept and receive God's grace and forgiveness, we also fail to give unconditional love and forgiveness to others. The result is a breakdown in our relationships with other people. And this is what causes emotional conflicts between us and those around us. The unforgiven are the unforgiving and the unforgiving complete the vicious circle because they cannot be forgiven. They are plagued with **guilt and resentment** which leads to the big three of **anxiety, stress, and depression.** And let me just add this: Perhaps the one you really need to forgive is yourself for some past sin.

5. Never hesitate to admit an error. It's a sign of maturity. James 5:16, "Confess your sins to each other and pray for each other so that you may be healed."

6. Respect the feelings of your husband or wife. He or she will remember this for a long time. Eph 5:33, "Each one of you also must love his wife as he loves himself and the wife must respect the husband."

7. Don't repay an insult with an insult. 1 Peter 3:9-10, "Do not repay evil with evil or insult with insult, but with blessing. Because to this you were called so that you may inherit a blessing. For, whoever would love life and seek good days must keep his tongue from evil and his lips from deceitful speech."

8. Remember that love covers over many errors. 1 Peter 4:8, "Above all love each other deeply because love covers over a multitude of sins."

9. A gentle answer turns away anger. Proverbs 15:1, "A gentle answer turns away wrath, but a harsh word stirs up anger."

10. A kind word spoken at just the right time is like apples of gold in settings of silver. Proverbs 25:11, "An idea well expressed is like a design of gold set in silver." (TEV)

11. Don't let the sun go down on your anger. Ephesians 4:26-27, "In your anger, do not sin. Do not let the sun go down while you are still angry and do not give the devil a foothold."

12. Don't whine! Philippians 2:14-15, "In everything you do, stay away from complaining and arguing so that no one can speak a word of blame against you."

13. Finally, once a year, make a list of everything for which you need to forgive your husband or wife and ask the Holy Spirit to help you to forgive him or her. Then, burn the list! Luke 6:37, "Do not judge and you will not be judged. Do not condemn and you will not be condemned. Forgive and you will be forgiven." We must all come to the realization that **God's forgiveness of our sins is conditional**, contrary to what you may have heard in the past. If you find yourself simply unable to forgive your husband or wife for some past sin, you need to understand that the Lord is not going to be able to forgive you for your past sins. We must all learn to wipe the slate clean of any bitterness that we may feel so that God will be able to wipe our slate clean.

Let me offer this closing bit of advice on resolving conflicts between wives and husbands, particularly if things have reached the point where your situation seems hopeless and you are considering separation or divorce. **Return to the beginning!** That is, return to the things you did when you first met each other. Remember that feeling you had when you first met and fell in love with each other and all the little things you did for one another while the passion of your romance was so strong. Try to remember those things, return to them, and start doing them again for each other.

I still believe in miracles! God is in the miracle business and I know that he can still work a miracle in your marriage if you are willing to put your trust in the Lord. Ask the Spirit of God to help you restore a right relationship with your husband or wife and also ask the Spirit to soften the heart of your husband or wife toward you. If you are willing to do these things, you may be surprised to find God doing a miracle in your life as well.

If either you or your spouse is suffering from low self-esteem, this will place tremendous added stress on your marriage and unfortunately statistics reveal that women are apparently much more vulnerable to suffering from feelings of inadequacy and low self-worth than are men. The young girl or boy who never quite measures up to her or his parent's expectations will have a life-long struggle with low self-esteem and will most likely carry a feeling of inadequacy with her or him unless the problem is addressed. I really think that Satan's deadliest weapon against us is low self-esteem. It is this feeling of inadequacy and inferiority that paralyzes our potential, ruins our relationships, and sabotages our Christian service. The trouble is that low self-esteem robs God of the opportunity to show the world his power and ability through our weaknesses. Too many of us believe that we can only bring glory to God when we are strong and can impress people. However, the apostle Paul claimed that there are only **two things which we can glory in.** The first, he said, is **the cross of Christ** (Gal 6:14). And the second is **our weaknesses** (2 Co 12-9-10). Why? Because God's strength is made perfect in our personal weaknesses and shortcomings. As believers, we are called to be healed helpers moving not out of strength but out of weakness.

If you are struggling with a poor self image, let me suggest two things which can help:

1. Ask God to check you every time you belittle yourself because you may find that your whole lifestyle is a direct or indirect putdown of yourself. For example, consider compliments. Are you able to accept a compliment comfortably without feeling the need to apologize?

2. Let God love you and let him teach you how to love yourself and your husband or wife. This involves surrendering your will to the Holy Spirit and asking for affirmation that you are a child of God and are worthy of God's love and affection.

I want to leave you with this final thought. If you desire to really experience the true happiness and fulfillment which God intends for your marriage, you and your husband or wife must **make the Holy Spirit the**

third partner in your marriage. As the Spirit leads you both into a deep and personal relationship with Christ and satisfies the spiritual hunger within each of you, so will your marriage bond be strengthened as you seek to love each other sacrificially, just as Christ loved the church. The real key to a happy marriage is found in Ephesians 5:21, **"Submit to one another out of reverence for Christ."** If yours is to be a Spirit-filled marriage, it is essential that you both follow Paul's admonition to submit or **yield to each other and cherish each other** out of a grateful heart for what the Lord has given to you.

~ Notes ~

~ Notes ~

www.ingramcontent.com/pod-product-compliance
Lightning Source LLC
Chambersburg PA
CBHW031254290426
44109CB00012B/578